DIVORCE PANIC

By Ralph Brewer

a.k.a "DSO"

helpformen.com

INTRODUCTION

Over the past several years of running Dad Starting Over and now Help For Men, I've coached and spoken one-on-one with well over one thousand guys. That still blows my mind. When I started offering my coaching services, I had no idea how popular it would become. There was such a need for my services that I had to hire help! The Help For men team now comprises SEVEN coaches: myself, five other guys from the United States, and one from Australia. I started an international men's group that includes online forums, live Zoom meetings, and one-on-one coaching.

Yes, we are extremely busy.

I'm not sharing all of this to brag, but to illustrate one main point:

YOU, MY FRIEND, ARE NOT ALONE. Not by a long shot.

There is a huge number of men out there who have had their lives suddenly uprooted. Some men got the dreaded "Dear John" letter as their wives packed their bags and ran away from their lives of boredom and responsibility. Other guys discovered that their wives were secretly having love affairs with one of the dads from their kids' soccer teams. Other men had to endure years of mental abuse at the hands of emotionally unstable women, only to have these women unexpectedly give up on the marriage and aggressively attack them in divorce court.

These men have one thing in common: They all say to themselves, "*This is NOT how it was supposed to end. We were supposed to grow old together. Kids. Grandkids. Great grandkids. We were supposed to be on the front porch sipping iced tea, enjoying our golden years. This… is not what I had planned. I don't understand why this is happening.*"

Welcome to the club that you never wanted to join. I was in your shoes a decade ago. You'll just have to trust me when I say that it gets better. Really. If you play your cards right, it can get downright amazing for you. You don't know it right now, but you have the potential to become an extremely high-value, single dude. As you will come to learn, the world is BEGGING for high-value men.

Years from now, you will look back on this time of your life as being extremely painful, awful, traumatic… and an absolutely necessary chapter in your storybook life. Every single, solitary great man that I have ever known has endured some kind of awful hardship in life. But they persevered. They overcame. They learned. They took that pain and anguish and turned it into something positive.

You may not see it right now, but you've just been given a gift. Yes, I know it looks like a giant steaming pile of dog shit right now… but buried deep in there is a diamond. You just have to do the awful and smelly work of digging in there to find it. You are worth the effort.

WHO THIS BOOK IS FOR

I wrote this book for heterosexual men that have endured a failed long-term relationship with a woman and are having a difficult time picking up the pieces and starting over in life. This book will appeal especially to those men who have discovered that their wives committed infidelity. For these men, life as they know it was completely turned upside down. I understand the confusion, the despair, and the anger that you are going through. I went through it all, too. You need a little help, a little boost, to help you understand it all and to get you up and over the wall. That's what this book is for.

Maybe there was no cheating. Maybe you just had a long-term partner that suddenly broke up with you and you're trying to understand what happened and how to successfully move forward in life. For you, consider this book a lesson in both why your breakup may have happened and how you can avoid a ton of trouble with the women in your future (yes, there will be more women). Learn from all of us who have been there and done that. An ounce of prevention is worth a pound of cure, as they say.

STEVE'S STORY

Steve's email to me was very typical for readers of my site at helpformen.com. All the situations are roughly the same, yet they all think they're unique in their own special blend of *"awful."* Steve, like many other readers, was convinced that the entire world was in on a cosmic joke at his expense. He feels like Jim Carrey's character from The Truman Show. Everyone is a cast member and the whole world is watching. He just pulled back the curtain and everything is finally starting to make sense. He doesn't like what he sees. In his mind, it was all just a big scam. Nothing was real.

Over the last few months, he has run the events that led him to this point again and again in his mind. He's trying to figure out where the marriage machine broke down. Dammit, he did everything by the fucking book and yet his marriage sure didn't go as planned. Not at all. He was promised a better life than this. He was promised the grandkids and the picket fence. He was promised comfort and stability. He did his part, goddammit, why didn't she??

 Now he's in an empty apartment, driving a shitty Toyota pickup truck that breaks down half the time, and he's only allowed to see his kids on Wednesdays after school and every other weekend. This really, really sucks, and it doesn't look like it's going to get better in the foreseeable future.

The TV show audience is now pointing and laughing at him. *"Haha!! He bought into the whole 'Til death do us part' thing?! Haha!! What a dumbass!"*

Steve is now a dangerous combination of angry, hurt, scared, and confused.

"I'M A GOOD GUY! I SWEAR!"

Most readers in Steve's shoes will immediately list all the positive stuff they did in their marriages. Steve was no different.

"I did laundry, I cooked, I cleaned, I did it all. I paid all the bills while she went into huge amounts of debt for her law degree. I didn't complain fucking once. I supported her in everything. She doesn't give a shit about anything I did for her!"

Steve was building up what I call a *"Good Provider"* resumé so that I wouldn't think he was some kind of abusive asshole loser like *"most other guys"* are. In his mind, he checked ALL of the *"good husband"* boxes. To think that his wife would even CONSIDER stepping outside of their marriage never even occurred to him, but that's exactly what she did. Multiple times.

The first time it happened, he saw text messages between her and a guy from one of her university classes. Steve had his suspicions. He saw her strange behavior going on for months. One evening, he finally got a hold of her phone and read every one of their messages to each other. He saw how the conversation and their relationship got progressively more sexual as time went on. He saw pictures they sent back and forth. First, they were innocent and friendly. Then that changed. Then it became full-fledged porn material.

He couldn't believe what he was looking at. THIS was his wife?!

He went to the internet for help. A quick Google search gave him pages and pages of results about cheating wives. Wow, people sure do cheat a lot. He read up on the growing phenomenon of *"emotional affairs"* happening thanks to social media and websites like Facebook. He read step-by-step guides for what to do when you catch your spouse cheating and he followed them to the letter. He approached his wife and her new emotional affair partner, threatened to expose them to everyone (including the lover's wife), and stopped the emotional affair dead in its tracks. Or so he thought. Later, he would learn that they simply moved the affair from the confines of Facebook to a seedy hotel on the other side of town. As is the case with such affairs, they rarely stay *"emotional"* for very long.

The wife's second affair occurred with an old boyfriend from her pre-marriage past. He was the quintessential "one that got away." For years, she would send innocent Facebook messages to him on every birthday and every Christmas, just so he wouldn't forget that she was still around. Steve knew about this ex-boyfriend, but he wasn't worried. This guy had his own wife and three kids, and he lived really far away. Besides, Steve was convinced that his wife's cheating days were well behind her. They both put in a lot of work over the years and really grew together as a couple. Through good times and bad, they were a team.

After one typical *"Merry Christmas!"* message from the wife
to the ex-boyfriend, the ex-boyfriend responded unusually.
"I really miss you," he said. That set off a chain reaction
in Steve's wife. Those old lustful feelings were back. Their
conversation went from sappy to sexual in no time. They
fondly reminisced about the dirty escapades they had
experienced all those years ago. Two hours into their heated
conversation, they made plans to meet. The ex-boyfriend
left his wife and kids for a *"business trip"* and drove six
hours to see Steve's wife. Steve's wife simply had to skip her
university classes for a day and Steve wouldn't know a thing
about it. She told a female classmate what she was up to, had
her take notes, and gave her a fake cover story to use in case
anyone asked where she was. She promised to pay her back
with lunch and drinks.

The two lovers spent hours reconnecting and having sex.
Old feelings came right back. They both envisioned a long
and wild affair that would give them much-needed relief
from their respective boring marriages and god-awful home
lives. They were both equally sick of screaming kids and the
dull spouses they lost attraction to years ago.

Unbeknownst to his wife, though, Steve knew ALL the
details of the secret affair. He had been tracking her exact
whereabouts and all of her online activity for weeks. Thanks
to everything he learned on the internet, he had the wisdom
to recognize his spouse's typical *"cheating wife"* behavior
and he immediately sprang into action. Steve became quite

the private investigator. His actions became obsessive. He confided in his friends about what was going on, and they all told him he was nuts and this was no way to live. His wife's emotional affair was years ago. Why can't he just let it go?

But, Steve's gut told him that something was up. He wasn't just being paranoid. He wasn't just exhibiting *"low self-esteem"* and *"obsessive-compulsive"* tendencies, as his therapist liked to tell him. He was sure that something was going on and he needed to get to the bottom of it.

Unfortunately, Steve ended up proving all of his friends wrong.

He gathered all the evidence and carried out his plan.

He informed the lover's spouse of the affair. He told the lover's employer why he missed work. He told officials at his wife's school that she was missing class and why. He met with an attorney and drew up a plan for splitting assets and debts. He immediately filed for divorce.

Unfortunately, Steve would learn what most men in his situation learn:

Nobody gives a shit.

His wife's lover kept his job. He's still married to the same woman. Nothing has changed for the man. His wife actually got angry when Steve called her with evidence of her husband's affair. She bluntly told him to stay out of her life and never contact her again. Steve would later learn that his wife's new lover was quite the player. This was not his first affair rodeo, and his wife stuck by him through it all. She apparently weighed the pros and cons of their marriage and decided it was worth the pain of dealing with his affairs.

The university administrative office never even replied to Steve's repeated emails and calls. His wife would later tell him she was friends with the office staff, and they laughed at him. They called him *"that psycho husband."* They couldn't care less about his wife's affair or that she was skipping classes. What does that have to do with them? As long as she keeps paying the bills for the classes, she could skip however many times she wants. After a while, they eventually returned his calls and let him know that his personal matters had nothing to do with the university and to please stop harassing them.

When it came time to divorce, it went a lot rougher than what Steve anticipated. His wife's family, the ones he considered the surrogate parents he loved with all his heart, cut off all contact with him. He considered this one of the largest acts of betrayal he had ever seen. *"Mom and dad"* abandoned him in favor of their "whore daughter." They stuck the knife in even further when they helped his wife pay for an attorney. A really good attorney. A really good attorney with a reputation for getting divorced moms a lot of money. The attorney would live up to his reputation.

Steve was painted as the villain in court documents. The

words *"abusive"* and *"neglect"* came up more than once. He was baffled. None of this was true. He was a good man. A good husband. A good father. Why would they do this to him?

Steve's own lawyer was nowhere near as well-seasoned as his wife's attorney. Yes, the wife's affair was brought up, but thanks to *"no fault"* laws, it had zero bearing on much of anything. Overall, it was just a matter of who should have the kids and when, who gets what asset, and who gets stuck with what bill.

At the end of the day, Steve was left in a small apartment on the opposite side of town with a growing stack of bills, half his 401k, zero savings, and a new drinking habit. Understandably, he feels that the world has just chewed him up and spit him out. The second he tried to make his case and prove his worth as a man, the world laughed at his naivety.

That's when Steve ended up on my website and shot me an email.

I patiently scrolled and read page after page of his first email to me. This is nothing new. I'm no longer shocked. I've officially heard it all. This is actually not THAT bad of a case compared to some I have read. At least, one of his ex-wife's mentally ill lovers didn't stab him nine times in the back and leave him to die like the other guy I recently talked to.

After a few emails back and forth, with Steve saying over

and over that this isn't how it was supposed to turn out, I grew a little impatient and said what I say to all guys in his position:

"Okay. You were wrong. So, now what?"

MY STORY

You hear it all the time: *"I remember it like it was yesterday."* It's true. With traumatic moments come crystal clear recollection. I remember all the sounds and smells of that day. This cruel photographic memory of traumatic events is there for a reason. I think of it as my brain's way of making sure I learned my lesson and never, ever forget what happened. Don't worry, brain. I won't forget. Lesson learned.

I was on the beach in sunny Florida with my wife and three kids. The weather was perfect. The kids were having a blast making sandcastles and running out into the ocean. Lots of laughs. That was a much-needed vacation for us. It's not like we had a really strenuous life back home. It was mostly what I would later call a very *"meh"* existence. We lived for the kids. We both worked a lot. That's about it. We were not a very intimate couple at all. We were basically buddies living under the same roof. The vacation in Florida was something different to take our minds off the banality of our existence. School, soccer games, work, housecleaning, basketball games, more work, wrestling meets, more work, more cleaning… that was our life. Being a parent can be a real drag, and something simple, like sitting on the beach and staring at the ocean, can make you feel alive again.

Our one-and-a-half-year-old baby boy was getting cranky. It was past his nap time. I volunteered to take the boy up to the condo while my wife stayed on the beach with the two older kids. I had injured my back earlier that day (something that happened to me all the time) and relaxing on the couch in the cool air-conditioning sounded really nice. I took the baby boy up, showered him off, put him to bed in fresh jammies, and lay down on the couch with the laptop to surf the web and possibly doze off.

I opened up the laptop and the first thing I saw was that the browser was open to Facebook. My wife was logged in. For some reason, and to this day I really don't know why, I decided to snoop. I went right to her private messages, and there it was: A brief snippet of a conversation between her and her personal trainer (yes, it's every bit as clichéd as it sounds). Their chat was sexual in nature, and obviously just a small part of a longer conversation. She had failed to delete these last few messages back and forth, but it was enough for me to see what was going on.

Was my wife having an affair? No fucking way.

I could go on and on about what happened next, but I will spare you the gory details. My marriage ended that day, and my wife was the one that thew in the dynamite and blew it all up. She filed for divorce right away. Life, as I knew it, was over.

Like most of you reading this, I tried to reconcile and keep the family together. Every single thing I did was wrong and just made the situation even worse. I should've just walked away with my head held high. I didn't. I groveled. I became even less of a man in her eyes and in the eyes of everyone around me. I was pitiful. I was pitiful at home, pitiful at work, and pitiful with friends. Nobody likes a pitiful man, as I was quick to learn. I lost a lot of respect from my social group during that time period and my relationships with them still aren't the same to this day.

My ex-wife was relieved that this deep dark secret of hers was finally out in the open, and she was free to start this new and exciting chapter of her life. As for me, I was left wondering what in the hell had just happened and where exactly I was supposed to go next. After all, everything about me revolved around my wife and my kids. I had zero family in the state we lived in. Hell, I had zero family in the entire country! All of my known blood relatives live over in Europe. I had a group of close friends, but they were all out of state. I left them behind when we moved to be closer to my wife's family — a mistake that I would come to regret.

Everybody I knew in our little town was because of my wife. I was friends with her coworkers and their spouses, but really nothing beyond that. I worked from home for much of my adult life, so I didn't have coworker friends to fall back on like my wife did. I was not, and I'm still not, what you would call a *"social butterfly."* I'm a writer. A creative guy. I do enjoy my measured doses of friend and party time. I can talk your head off, but I also enjoy my alone time. It keeps me sane. Ironically, that all went right out the fucking window with divorce.

I ended up with my kids four to five days a week, depending upon my ex's *"work"* schedule. Whether I had the temperament for the job didn't really matter. I was now mom AND dad. For my ex, being a divorced mom with a new boyfriend took up a tremendous amount of her time and energy. It's hard to shoehorn kid time into your life when you're busy playing the mating game with a new partner. Her solution, more often than not, was to just leave the kids alone at her house, with friends, or with me. Being in love can make you do some stupid things, as we all know.

After the divorce, my ex became a completely new human being. That is not at all an exaggeration. There is very little of the woman I knew for twenty years still there. Physically, she is a new human, and behaviorally, she's an exaggeration of all the negatives she and I both used to despise. She became exactly what she said she always hated. I would learn that this is common amongst broken adulterous women.

Was this person we see now always in there, lurking away in the shadows of her psychological baggage? Was the person I knew and loved just a facade all those years? Was she really molded and shaped that easily by her new man? What in the hell happened to my best friend?

In hindsight, I did a really shitty job of properly vetting my wife candidate. I let too much crap slip through the cracks over the years. I ignored the obvious red flags for the sake of being a faithful husband. Yes, we ended up having three beautiful children together and I love them with all of my heart… but the results of my poor marital decisions are showing themselves beyond just a cheating ex-wife and a divorce. My children will have to endure the emotional scars and trauma associated with a mom who picked up and left during the crucial stages of their adolescent development.

Since going through this awful chapter of my life, I have learned a great deal about the relationship game, about starting over, and about myself. Going through it has been hell, but I wouldn't change anything. The pain has been a great learning experience and has helped shape me into the man I am today.

Much like my ex-wife, I am a completely different human being now… but in a good way. There is very little of the old me left.

Good riddance, I say. He was a dumb fuck, anyway.

CHAPTER 1
IT'S OVER

DID YOU CATCH YOUR WIFE CHEATING ON YOU?

Maybe she just suddenly asked for some *"space"* or a *"relationship timeout"* so that she can think clearly about your future together? Maybe she needs to go away and *"find"* herself. Did she say, *"I just don't have feelings for you anymore,"* or, *"I love you but I'm not IN LOVE with you anymore"*? Did she just ask you for an open relationship?

Sorry, my man. It's over. These are the typical signs of a cheating wife, or at the very least a wife who has checked out of the relationship completely due to some outside circumstance. She has probably detached from you and latched onto another human being, or something has caused her to have a drastic shift in her attitude towards your marriage. Once that happens, there is no going back to your old life. The partner you knew and loved is dead.

I know, you can't believe it. You refuse to believe it. You don't want life as you knew it to be over. Not like this. It's all just happening way too fast for you to comprehend. I know you probably hold on to a glimmer of hope that your relationship with your ex will rekindle, and it will be as strong as ever. You probably have fantasies of your ex *"waking up"* from this crazy, irrational stupor she is in and suddenly remembering what a great couple you are. She will recognize the value in the life you have built together over all these years.

"I don't know what I was thinking. I love you!! Let's start over again!"

It's not going to happen. It's over.

There are lots of friends, therapists and others that will sell you on the dream of reconciliation. I'm not one of them. I have literally never seen reconciliation succeed long-term after a wife's affair. It's most likely just not going to happen to you. I'm sorry. I know it sucks and you don't want to believe it, but it's the truth. That's what you need right now: the truth. You don't need somebody else blowing smoke up your ass. All that does is lead you to wasting much of your precious time on Earth chasing your tail. It will lead you to nowhere but additional heartache and a deep depression.

Oh sure, there are stories out there of the wayward ex-wife crawling back to the husband. It happens.

She may be tearful. She may be remorseful. She may be beyond regretful for the mistakes she has made. She may do her absolute best to convince you, the betrayed man, that she has learned from her mistakes and will never do those bad things ever again for as long as you both shall live. She may, in fact, believe every single word of it herself.

Either consciously or unconsciously… she's lying about her future with you.

She will either still be continuing on with her destructive behavior in a more secretive way (with affairs, they rarely ever break contact completely with their affair partners), or she will just start all over again with somebody or something else in the near future. How do I know? Because I've seen this scenario played out hundreds of times, and I've never seen reconciliation work after a wife so vigorously detaches from her man. Never. Why?

Your wife is now an addict.

Your wife is now an affair junky. She just got a taste of the high that only a new sexual relationship can offer. She just took a potent shot of sexual heroin. There's no going back now. No other drug on the planet compares to the thrill of a new lover. Your long-term, comfortable relationship can't hold a candle to the feelings that a secret affair can bring about. Even the love for her own kids doesn't compare to the overwhelming nature of an affair. These new feelings of hers are a completely different ballgame.

Unfortunately, like all other addicts, she has to hit rock bottom before she sees the light and MAYBE gets better (this usually coincides with multiple failed affairs and her advancing age). You don't want to be around for rock bottom, trust me. Broken women usually take their man and everyone else down with them. It's not a pretty picture.

Let the relationship die. It's for the better. You will be okay. Trust me.

I know this feeling of loss hurts worse than anything you've ever felt. As several military veterans have told me:

"I was in active-duty combat. I saw my friends get killed. I was hit by an IED. I've endured months of physical and mental therapy to just get back to normal. None of that compares to the pain I feel right now with this divorce."

This divorce stuff… it sucks. Bad. Why is it so damn painful? Well, going back to the drug analogy for a moment:

You're addicted to your wife.

You're not necessarily addicted in an unhealthy, codependent kind of way, but you're still addicted. You have been emotionally attached to this person for YEARS. You've been through EVERYTHING together. You've seen good times and bad. You've been there to support each other through it all. You were there for her during her breast cancer scare, and she was there when your dad died. You have years of inside jokes, stories, and memories that will last you a lifetime. She was there when you woke up, and she was there when you went to bed. Every day. For years.

For all of this to suddenly GO AWAY is traumatic. It's like losing a limb. You're still reaching over and trying to touch an arm that is no longer there. You still feel the phantom pain and tingles… but… nothing.

Somebody has taken away your drug. It's like being a heroin addict. Take away their needles and drugs, and in no time, they feel like they want to die. The drugs don't make them feel high anymore. They just make them feel NORMAL. Without the drug, they are sweating and shaking profusely. They feel like they're going to vomit.

They're addicted, and so are you.

I can't tell you how many times I've heard from men that have read my books, "Dude. It's like you were sitting in my house watching me! This is creepy!" So, how is that possible? How do we all have such similar experiences? Why are our thoughts and reactions to this kind of trauma so damn similar?

Because… as I'll keep referencing in this book, **Mother Nature is a real bitch.**

WE ARE ENGINEERED TO BECOME ADDICTED TO OUR ROMANTIC PARTNERS

Mother Nature has one big goal in mind: To get you to make babies and help take care of them. That's about it. Everything you work towards in life, the more you think about it, is to achieve the goal of propagating the human species. Part of our instincts, as men, is to spread our seed far and wide and get our unique DNA out there in the world. Mother Nature recognizes that she has planted this lustful desire in us, so she counteracts that desire with the need to BOND and form real relationships with women.

In other words, Mother Nature makes us fall in love.

From what I can gather based on the men I have talked to over the years, men tend to be the romantics in relationships. We are ready to sacrifice our lives for the women we love. We will go to war for them. We will do whatever we can to protect them. Sure, we lust after them and our eye seems to wander from time to time, but we also have a deep-down desire to take care of and cherish this human female we call *"wife."*

That is our commitment. Our devotion. Our love.

When the relationship machine clicks like it should, nothing on the planet feels better. For many of us, we get that initial *"in love"* high in a VERY extreme dose at the early stages of the relationship. This high is so potent that the memory of it carries us through the years of what later becomes a pretty boring relationship. Many men have experienced the dreadful ache of the dull long-term marriage, only to have their energy reawakened by a wife who wears that special dress they love so much… and he is instantly taken back to that special weekend away in Cabo they had twenty years ago.

It's like his wife is the lone dealer for the drug that he desperately needs to feel *"normal"* again. He doesn't need his drug on a daily basis. Just enough to keep the shakes and nausea from kicking in.

Many women are acutely aware of the power they possess in relationships. You'll hear women joke about it with their girlfriends. *"My husband was super grumpy all week. His work was killing him. Then I remembered we didn't have sex for the past two weeks. I just had to give him that look, and he was attacking me in the bedroom. He'll be all better for a couple more weeks. Men are so stupid."*

We're not stupid, we're human. We need that sexual release, that validation, and that connection with a woman that says, at a very visceral level, *"You have value. You are a desirable man. I care about you."* We need our drug.

Without it… it's not a good thing.

That's why men do some pretty desperate things to hang on to their drug.

STOP CHASING

I know you're not feeling very well at the moment. If you're one of the bazillions of guys who have discovered your wife's affair, you are feeling especially shitty right now. Depressed. Angry. Confused. Intensely sad.

Totally understandable.

Whether it's a sudden, unexplained divorce filing, or the discovery of an affair and all the dirty details that go with it, you are feeling a sense of betrayal. For men, that betrayal is especially harsh and difficult to deal with. It's tough for us guys to be vulnerable with others, and when somebody takes advantage of that vulnerability or our *"nice"* behavior, we want to lash out and punish the world.

Infidelity is especially bad because it calls into question the three main facets of your existence:

Your present. *"Are we still a couple? Does she love me? Why is she acting this way? Why is she saying these things?"*

Your future. *"What does this mean for us moving forward? What will my life look like five years from now?? Will I be a single guy again? What do I know about dating?!"*

Your past. *"Wait... does that mean that the weird thing she did last year was because of this affair? Did she say that one thing because she had fallen in love with the other guy? That was three years ago! She said they just met last year. Is she* *lying about all the stuff back then, too?"*

It's all just one giant mind fuck. It hurts. Continuously. You are in withdrawal.

You know what one surefire way to fix all this pain is? To get your drug back! If you get HER back, all of this misery will go away, right?

So you push. You pressure. You write her long text messages. Emails. Voicemail messages. You talk to her friends. You talk to her family.   You threaten her affair partner. You try to enlist the help of every loved one you can think of. You must try and convince your wife that she needs to just stop being a crazy woman. She must go back to being your loving wife. You want to do ALL you can to stop the ship from sinking.

Everyone should applaud this type of behavior, right? Everyone should see all of your actions as coming from a caring and loving husband who wants to save his marriage. This should be the prescription necessary for turning this situation around, right?

Actually, it just makes everything worse.

When a woman ends her relationship with a man, either via an affair or just the gradual loss of love and affection, she has signaled her loss of respect. In her life movie, the part of husband/partner is now empty or has been filled by somebody else. This lack of respect also usually coincides with a very real disdain for the man. Sometimes the man is seen as pitiful. The wife may say to herself, *"I feel bad for ruining this guy's life. He's a good father and a good man… I just can't stomach the idea of being his wife anymore."* That's the best-case scenario. The worst, and most common case is, *"This guy is getting in the way of me realizing my real self. I haven't felt this great in I don't know how long, and it's all because I have detached from him. He needs to get the hell out of my way, or I will lose my fucking mind."*

Either way, actively pursuing and trying to win back the heart of your wayward or disconnected wife… it will not win you any points, not with your wife, your friends, or your family. At best, it will further lower her respect for you. At worst, it will turn you into the worst possible enemy imaginable, and she will make it her life's work to ruin you. After all, you are actively getting in the way of her happiness.

What the man in this scenario should do is hold his head high, do his crying and screaming in private, tell the soon-to-be ex that he understands and wishes her the best… and then immediately go into business mode. When a wife detaches from her man, that's when the romantic relationship ends, and the business relationship begins. At that point, it's a matter of going through the logistics of the split. That's the best plan for the finances, for the mutual property, and for the mental health of the husband who was caught completely off guard.

The worst thing possible for the man is to hold out hope,

chase the wife, beg the wife, grovel to all of those around him, and continue pursuing, even when repeatedly pushed away.

As the author Mark Manson once stated, in any kind of personal relationship you enter into, you want the other person's reaction to you to be a *"FUCK YES!"* If you ask your friend to go into business with you, you don't want a *"Man… I dunno. Maybe. I'll have to think about it. I'll get back to you."* You want to hear, *"Fuck yes! I was hoping you would ask! I have some plans already written down for how to make some more money!"* That's the energy that shows you the other person will be committed. They will bring the energy that will lead to success. That guy is a winner of a partner. To hear, *"Man… I dunno. Maybe,"* means that he doesn't see the real potential in you and/or your business idea. He's basically saying, *"I think there are better options for me out there."*

When you are in a failed romantic relationship with somebody, you don't want to chase, beg, plead, and campaign to win them back. You're never going to get a *"Fuck yes"* from them. They've already been sold on Plan B as being the better option.

But let's play pretend for a moment. Let's say that you play the game and do the little dance anyway. Here is the absolute best-case scenario ahead of you:

Because of your actions, and hopefully some sense of right and wrong in her own mind, she has genuine remorse for all she has done wrong. She wants to work hard to figure out why she did this bad thing to you. She officially takes divorce off the table. She tears up the paperwork and vows to never bring up the subject again. If she's a cheater, she calls her affair partner on the phone in front of you and tells him they are over. She calls her family and confesses all she has done wrong. She grovels and begs for your forgiveness. She drops to her knees and performs every sex act imaginable on you (sorry to be crass… but many guys reading this are nodding their heads because they've seen this exact scenario play out).

Sounds great, right?

But then, she later does that thing that makes you question her behavior. *"Who were you texting just now?"* you ask. *"Why were you fifteen minutes late from work?"* She will grow tired of your anxiety-driven interrogations. Your marriage therapist will tell your wife that she needs to be patient with you as you work through the trauma. This is part of the healing process.

The recent wild sex you experienced was only temporary. You'll learn that this is a common psychological phenomenon known as *"hysterical bonding."* It's a short-lived period of extreme closeness and intimacy that usually follows affairs. When that stage of the reconciliation fades and you feel your wife pulling away, you'll get needy. Is she taking your drug away again?! Nope, she's just going back to the old her. The old her was not sexually aroused by her husband. *"This will take lots of work to get past,"* the marriage therapist tells you. *"You need to be patient with her."*

You'll notice that your wife's demeanor towards you will grow worse with time. It's almost like she has a deep-down level of disdain for you. She seems resentful over… what, exactly? Is she mad because you love her too damn much? Shouldn't she be grateful to have a guy who works so hard to keep her around? After all, she was the one to do those bad things and try to end the marriage!

But no, the distance grows and grows. Again, best-case scenario, you just go through the motions. You take care of kids, the house, and on those rare occasions where she has a little too much to drink and the kids are staying at grandma's house, she'll show you some of that old validation and the physical/emotional connection you crave… but only for a fleeting moment. Ninety percent of the time you are in a state of disconnected *"Blah."* After much reflection, you'll realize that this has been the state of your relationship for years. Even before the whole divorce and affair thing, your marriage was just… shitty.

You'll have the epiphany that many guys in this position have:

"What was I fighting for, exactly?"

But, if you're like most guys I talk to, you'll stick it out. You hold on to the hope that ONE DAY you'll get back to that high you felt when you got that potent shot of new

relationship energy you felt so many years ago. Your drug
is in there, you tell yourself, you just have to wait it out and
work even harder to find it.

It doesn't work.

It's hard to get to that feel-good new relationship drug state
when you're in a long-term healthy relationship. It's damn
near impossible when your partner has emotionally and
physically disconnected from you. It is, by my estimation,
completely impossible after they have latched onto and pair-
bonded with another man.

You're just chasing your tail. You'll never catch it.

Stop chasing. Your wife is no longer your drug dealer. I
know it hurts. The withdrawal is a real bitch. You can and
will get over it.

DAVE'S STORY

Dave booked a one-on-one session with me after reading my book, The Dead Bedroom Fix. I read his pre-meeting summary, and I was a bit confused. He read my book about how to restart sex within your marriage… but his situation didn't really call for a dead bedroom fix. His situation was what I routinely call a *"raging dumpster fire."*

• Dave dated a woman with a six-month-old child.

• Dave let them move in with him just two months after dating.

• Dave married the woman three months after that.

• Soon after marriage, sex with his new bride stopped.

• She spent every waking moment on her phone.

• She would routinely go out with friends and leave him to watch *"their baby."*

• When she was home, she was angry.

• They were in a completely sexless marriage for a full year.

• He discovered she was texting other men.

• A friend of his said that he heard his wife was hanging all over other men at a bar (while Dave was watching *"their baby"*).

• His wife eventually said, *"I love you, but I'm not in love with you."*

• She brought up divorce after only a year and a half of marriage.

After all the above happened to Dave, his solution was to go on the internet and search for… *"how to fix a sexless marriage."* That's how he found me, my books, and scheduled the coaching session.

He ignored the fact that he dated a new mother, had her move in right away, married her, watched every red flag imaginable once married, watched her probable cheating, etc.… No, his biggest pain point, as far as he was concerned, was his lack of sex.

Dave's story is NOT unique. I wish it was, but it's not. He got himself into a horrible mess and he's still not clear on HOW it all happened. As far as he's concerned, everything would be fine if they just had sex again.

Me: *"Dude… your wife is cheating on you and asked for divorce. Sorry to be so blunt. This isn't a dead bedroom issue. You're well beyond that."*

Dave: *"First of all, I don't know for a fact that she's cheating. I know everyone says that, but I don't have real proof yet. I've looked through her phone, but she keeps erasing messages.*

I put a tracker on her car, but it doesn't work right. If I just had more evidence, I would agree and leave. I don't just quit because my friends and you think she's cheating."

Dave is probably what your psychologist types would call a *"codependent"* person, and his issues probably all started in childhood. After additional coaching sessions, we would eventually uncover that yes, his childhood was very messed up. His dear mother and absent father both did a real number on poor Dave.

I tell Dave what I tell every guy in his situation: *"Your marriage is over. You need to concentrate on YOU for a change. Figure out what got you in this mess. Why are you so attracted to women like this and why do you stick around when it's obviously so terrible? That's your big goal right now. Internal work. It's the hardest but most rewarding work, by far. Whatever you do, please stay away from women for a while."*

Dave: *"Oh, you don't have to worry about that. I have no interest in women. Trust me. I have a lot of stuff I need to work on."*

By our next session, Dave would admit to starting up an online dating account and right away clicking with a girl who *"seems very normal!"* I hung my head and sighed. I knew how this was going to end. Most guys do exactly what Dave did… and it never ever ends well.

I never heard from Dave again after that chat about his new girlfriend. He still has two sessions on the books that he has never used. That's also not unusual.

39

CHAPTER 2
WHY DID THIS HAPPEN?

WHY DID THIS HAPPEN TO YOU? THAT'S THE MILLION DOLLAR QUESTION WE ALL WANT THE ANSWER TO, RIGHT?

What could you have done to prevent this? WHY on Earth did your wife detach from you like this? Why is she so hell-bent on destroying you and the family you have built together over all these years? Has she forgotten all the wonderful things you've done together? What about all the memories you made together? How can she so easily discard *"us"* like this? Is this just how it is with most women after years of marriage?

Why do we stress ourselves out with these questions over and over in our minds? Well, it's a perfectly natural part of the common grieving process for men. If you want to shoehorn it into the five common stages of grief (denial, anger, bargaining, depression, and acceptance), it would probably fall under the *"bargaining"* category. It's a way for men to digest the trauma and eventually come to terms with the reality of the situation. For most men who have discovered an affair, there's an intense period of trying to make everything go back to the way it was before. Men are fixers, after all. We HAVE to figure out how and why the relationship machine broke down so suddenly, and what we can do to repair it and prevent it from ever happening again.

Contrary to what many men on the internet will tell you, the overall reason for the wife's disconnection and subsequent divorce is not as simple as, *"She's just a whore. All women are."* Sure, there are a ton of websites, forums, articles and angry male friends out there that will quickly use the *"all women are like that"* (AWALT) excuse as the explanation for what seems to be an epidemic of "walk-away-wife" behavior in the modern world. Creating such a convenient excuse is a nice and simple way for you to place your anger at the feet of the opposite gender. You can wipe your hands of all responsibility and stop digging any further for the truth. It also feels nice to stick the proverbial knife deep into the person who hurt you so badly. What better way to hurt them than to say that they are just inherently EVIL and FLAWED to the core? They're cursed because they are a WOMAN and there's nothing she can do to stop being so awful.

So… then what's the complete truth here? Well, it's not so simple. The more you learn and dig into the alarming stats (some studies show that 80% of divorces are initiated by women), the more complex and nuanced the situation becomes. I will try my best to break down what I feel contributes to this awful phenomenon that you have been unwittingly placed into.

WE'VE REMOVED MANY OF THE CONSTRAINTS AROUND MARRIAGE

You'll often hear men, mostly your more "conservative" men, talk about the *"good old days."* They'll talk about how women *"just aren't the same anymore."* It used to be that you could *"count on a woman,"* they will say. Women had *"honor"* and were far more *"devoted"* to their men. The wife stayed at home, and the husband worked. The system, by default, generated a great deal of respect for the man in the relationship because he was the provider. He was delegated the majority of the authority in the relationship. *"Don't bother dad, he's tired from work,"* the mom would say as she prepared dinner and made her husband a stiff drink.

Well, did we really think that would last very long?

We had our moment, guys, and then the women woke up. The entire frame around the concept of *"marriage"* and *"partnership"* was flipped upside down. Suddenly the woman can control her reproduction with a little but powerful thing call the *"birth control pill."* As we would later learn, telling women that: *"You can have sex freely like a man does without worry of getting pregnant"* was not without its consequences. I could go on for a few more chapters about how that little pill changed the sexual landscape… but let's just say it was freaking huge.

On top of the medical advances, we also had major advances in how society promotes women in the workforce. Women now make up the majority of our college students. Women are rising in the corporate ranks. Women are making partner in law firms. Go to any graduating class in the world of optometry, pediatrics, and other high-paying medical fields, and you will see an ocean of women ready to enter the workforce.

WOMEN ARE BRINGING HOME THE BACON… AND OH BOY, HAS THAT CHANGED EVERYTHING

We now have millions of self-sustaining women changing the parameters for what makes a *"good man"* that they will commit to. The checklist used to be pretty short: *"Make decent money so that you can take care of me and our future children… oh, and be a decent human being, too."* Now, the list includes things like:

• *"Make more money than me. I need to admire and respect my partner. Oh, by the way, I make more than probably 99% of the people you know."*

• *"Be my lover. Since I really don't NEED your money and financial support, you need to provide for me in other ways. Excite me. Give me something to look forward to on a daily basis."*

• *"I need a real man. Somebody who will stick up to me occasionally. Somebody who can take care of himself and me in case things get scary. I need to lean on my man. I need the knight in shining armor."*

• *"Don't be needy. I can't stand an overly emotional guy who needs me all the damn time. I don't have time for that. Yuck."*

So, reading over this list… you may say to yourself, *"Yeah, good luck, ladies! You will not find that guy!"* Exactly. Why do you think there are so many news articles with titles like, *"Where Have all the Good Men Gone?!"* Newsflash, the men haven't changed. They have remained the same. Which is precisely part of the problem.

The rules of the relationship game have changed, and many of you have been completely caught off guard.

This same changing paradigm applies not just to the dating world, but also to the world of marriage. If your woman is gainfully employed and can completely take care of herself without you, you better believe she looks at you differently than if she were a 1950s housewife in the kitchen with an apron and a kid on her hip. The more her paycheck goes up, the more the paradigm shifts… whether you know it or not.

Let's say, if you're like a lot of guys that I talk to, you're still running your marriage on the old principle of *"wife is a stay-at-home mom while husband works"*. Great. Good for you! BUT… please keep one thing in mind: You're not *"safer"* than the other guy who is married to the heart surgeon. Your wife could have an epiphany and decide to leave you, and you'll be left paying a hefty lump sum every month in the form of state-sanctioned child support and possibly alimony. As many men quickly learn, even if the wife cheats and steals her way out of a marriage, the courts will usually still reward her with a hefty judgment in her favor. In the state's mind, they are not punishing the dad… but doing what is best for the children and the mother who "sacrificed" her earning potential to care for a home and children.

ON TOP OF THE SHIFTING FINANCIALS OF MARRIAGE AND DIVORCE, THERE IS THE DWINDLING SOCIAL STIGMA OF DIVORCE

What used to be a very hush-hush topic around the office water cooler is now as innocuous as talking about the weather or the game on TV last night.

Guy #1: *"Oh yeah, did you hear? Gary and Sandy are getting divorced. She filed last week. She's already dating that Steven dude in accounting… you know, the one we thought she was flirting with…"*

Guy #2: *"Damn. Well, saw that coming. Hope Gary doesn't get screwed too bad."*

Guy #1: *"Yeah, looks like she's going after the house and wants the kids most of the time."*

Guy #2: *"Ugh… sucks. You try those new Doritos that just came out?"*

Divorce is no big deal. It's about as exciting as watching paint dry. This is something that a lot of men have a hard time coming to grips with. They see their friends treat their adulterous wayward wives as… just normal friends. Their friends don't see them as the social outcasts that he feels they SHOULD be. They should be ignoring their Facebook posts and text messages, but instead they're setting them up with some cheap furniture for their new apartments and inviting them over for their normal Friday barbecues.

"Nobody cares that she cheated and ruined our family?!" No, my man, they don't care. They still see your ex as a friend. Sure, a friend that did something stupid and hurt their other friend, but they see that as a personal family matter, and not something that affects their day-to-day lives. They have jobs, kids, and lots of other crap to worry about. "Sally cheated on John and filed for divorce" is a juicy piece of gossip, for sure, but it quickly gets set aside for things like preparing for little Timmy's out-of-town soccer tournament next weekend.

SO, TO RECAP...

1. Women today are making more money than ever before. A lot of these women realize that they no longer need a man for monetary purposes… but they still require that their men be higher than them on the social food chain (by way of money and/or status). If that doesn't happen… then the man is no longer needed. Not always, of course, but it's enough of a trend that economists have noticed and started to worry.

2. If the woman doesn't make more money than the man, she can still leave, and the state will require that the man pay her a great deal of money and half of his assets. So, in

either scenario, the foundation of financial safety is there.

3. The social stigma and forbidden nature of divorce is gone. Nobody cares. It's not a big deal. Your ex will not be shamed for blowing up the marriage.

That's a pretty potent three-punch combo that puts a real dent in the institution of marriage. No wonder it fails so often!

So, are we saying then that the high marriage success rates of the past were based on the fact that women NEED-ED men to survive and that the state didn't reward her so heavily if she divorced her man? Did it also help that society shamed her for being a divorced single mom?

Seems to be that way, doesn't it?

Does that mean that marriage, as we all know it, doesn't exist unless we FORCE it to exist by putting unnatural, and possibly unfair constraints around the whole institution, and around women in particular?

Well, marriage, as an institution, will probably always exist… but just not for most of us. Perhaps marriage and kids are, at least on paper, a pretty nice way to keep our society humming along smoothly. It keeps men and women from wandering, it gives children a stable home to grow in, and it also has tremendous benefits for our economy. Unfortunately, like many things *"on paper,"* real-world results seen out in the field can differ dramatically from the intended results.

MODERN-DAY MARRIAGE ISN'T FOR EVERYONE

Let's get this out of the way: Yes, I married again. After all the bullshit that I went through and all the horror stories I've heard from over one thousand men, I married for the second time. WHY? Well, I believe in the institution of marriage and long-term monogamy. I believe in it for ME. Before you throw down this book in disgust, hear me out.

WE HAVE OVERSOLD MARRIAGE

The modern-day concept of marriage is not for most of us. It can be argued that marriage is a VERY unnatural state for humans to be in. Just from a very visceral, animalistic perspective, it doesn't make biological sense. Therefore, we need some serious rules and constraints around the construct of marriage if we want to make it work for most people. Remove those rules and constraints… and hello rising divorce rate!

Therefore, if you want to put together a couple that will go through life personifying *"until death do us part,"* they both need to have a certain set of skills and personalities that lend themselves to being monogamous and happy in today's society. Those types of people exist, but they are NOT the majority of us. Not by a longshot.

That doesn't make non-marriage types BAD or *"sub-optimal"* in the human species, it just means that they don't have the right tools in their toolboxes for that particular job. Think of a bunch of animals at an Olympic pool all lined up to swim against each other in a big race. You have some dolphins, sharks, a koala, a panda bear, and a human. The dolphin and shark will leave everyone else behind. The human will keep up for a bit, but not long. The koala and panda will fall in the water and then scream until somebody saves them.

Does that mean that koalas and pandas are just all-around terrible animals, and we should take them outside and shoot them? No! The koalas and pandas do their own special thing in life. Just because they can't swim doesn't mean they don't have value. They're adorable! Who doesn't want to hug a panda?!

In fact, most of the animals in the animal kingdom wouldn't be able to compete with dolphins and sharks in a swimming race. That doesn't mean that our value as slow or non-swimming animals is nil. We do PLENTY of other things that give us a purpose in life.

For many reasons, though, most of us have been sold on the concept that marriage is the absolute pinnacle of existence. Without marriage, some of your more conservative-minded people might say, society will crumble! They may very well have a point, but which group of people will create order, and which will create chaos? The people who have the upfront skills and desire to be married? Or those who feel obligated to marry, despite their obvious inadequacies, and attempt to just learn as they go?

I've spoken to A LOT of men over the years, and I can tell you that most of the guys that are dealing with a toxic marriage also endured a toxic childhood. Their moms and dads weren't wired for the marriage thing, the kids sat back and watched the disaster unfold, and now those kids pass that particular flavor of *"relationship skills"* (or lack thereof) down to their own kids. The cycle will continue for generations. All of that could have been stopped if one of them just asked, *"Wait... do I really HAVE to be married? Can't I just hold off for a bit?"*

In some people's eyes, to even utter such a thought is blasphemous. To be single at a certain advanced age is seen as suspicious. *"Something must be WRONG with her,"* they will say about Aunt Brenda who lives alone with her pets. *"No wife... not sure you can't trust him,"* management will say about the thirty-five-year-old guy they are considering for promotion (I've heard these exact words said in a corporate meeting years ago). The message is obvious. Not only is marriage the ideal framework for life, but it is expected. If you don't do the whole marriage thing, something must be seriously wrong with you.

This, I contend, has gotten many of us into a whole heap of trouble.

Well, who exactly should and shouldn't tie the knot? Well, part of me says, *"Who the hell am I to say?"* Another part of me recognizes that I have years of personal and second-hand wisdom that most definitely provide a valuable perspective on this whole *"marriage"* debate.

After so many coaching sessions with readers and followers of Dad Starting Over and Help For Men, I notice patterns. There are certain types of men and women that fail at this marriage game. It's gotten to where I can finish stories for my clients. *"Dude… how did you know?! It's like you were there,"* they will often say. It's not because I'm some kind of psychic medium. I've just learned over the years how disturbingly predictable people can be in the relationship game.

To better illustrate, let's break this down into common scenarios and personalities that I see from the male and female side of the failed marriage fence.

MR. PLAYBOY

As a man, it can be argued that I am physically engineered to bang and impregnate lots of different women in my lifetime. We men make millions of sperm. We have been imprinted with a level of sexual desire that our female counterparts cannot fathom. Sure, women can be horny and run off with the pool boy for a wild romp in the hay, but they can't reach the consistent level of *"holy shit"* horny that most of us men experience on a daily basis.

Some men I talk to say that the notion that men have such a high sex drive is way overblown. *"We're not all horndogs,"* they say. *"We're not animals."* To them, I say that the evidence overwhelmingly proves one thing over and over:

There is an enormous population of men that aren't getting all the sexual gratification they need, so they look outside of their relationships to fill their sexual coffers.

Prostitution is called *"the world's oldest profession"* for a reason. Since the concept of exchanging money for services was conceived, people put women and sex out on the market for men to buy. Yes, for MEN to buy. I'm sure somewhere at some place in time, a woman has purchased the services of a prostitute, but that is laughably rare compared to men. As a man, you can go to any bad part of any major city, pull your car up to a corner, and some woman will come up to you and ask you if you're looking for a good time. She will offer to perform sexual favors for you in exchange for your money. Now, be a woman parking in the same spot in the same city. The closest thing she'll get to the same experience is some scary-looking guy offering HER money to sleep with HIM.

Pornography is rampant. I can go online and find an endless supply of porn videos to watch… all completely free. I may have to watch an advertisement, but that's about it. I will never run out of completely-free porn from now until the day I die. They just keep making new videos. With that being said, porn is still a multi-billion-dollar industry. How? Because there are companies and independent women online selling *"special"* porn that goes outside of the limits of what the free porn can offer. Millions of men all over the world fork over money for the pay-for-porn, even when the free stuff is so readily available.

I could go on and on about strip clubs, massage parlors, the rate of infidelity in married men… but here's a personal story to illustrate the power of the male sex drive, especially at the early stages of a new relationship:

One night, soon after a fancy shmancy invitation-only, outdoor farm-to-table seven-course dinner with my wife, my body decided that it needed to hastily evacuate my stomach and all of its expensive hipster-prepared contents. Not sure if it was food poisoning or a virus that I caught from the kids, but I experienced eight straight grueling hours of explosive vomiting and butt-torturing diarrhea. It was not pretty.

As the sun came up the next day, my body was finally done punishing me. I lay in bed a dehydrated and broken shell of a man. It felt like I had been through war. My girlfriend (future wife) laid down next to me, naked after a shower. I took one look at her, and my penis took over. I had to have her. She couldn't believe I could conjure up the energy to get the deed done, but I did. There was no work on her part needed to get me into the right head space necessary to have sex with her right then and there (beyond being naked next to me). I saw her body, and I wanted her. She was willing. Done. We had sex. It didn't matter that I had spent the entire night staring at a toilet filled with the foulest concoction a mind can conjure up. It didn't matter that my muscles were cramping, and my lips were dry from dehydration. The only thing that mattered was my penis saying, *"Hey, boss. See that over there? Any particular reason why you're not letting me do my job right now?"*

So, as far as men are concerned, to take that level of sexual desire and then point to one woman and say, *"SHE will be the only person you have intimate relations with from now until the day you die… AND as you guys grow older together, she's going to want it less and less, BUT your desire will probably remain pretty consistent."* Well… that doesn't sound very attractive to a sizeable chunk of the male population. For some men I talk to, the ones that I call *"Mr. Playboy,"* they had wild and crazy years doing whatever the hell they wanted to do and filled with dozens and dozens of sexy women all willing to jump on their train. That level of physical validation is extremely intoxicating for men. Beyond addictive. After all, that seems to be what we are engineered to do, yet only a select few of us can achieve it! But, eventually these guys grow tired of the conga line of easy women, and they want to settle down with a "good" wife and some kids. They're tired of the shallow world of easy sex and late-night clubbing. Or so they tell themselves…

It doesn't take many years into the relationship, usually after kids come into the picture, to get to where the man slowly realizes that the honeymoon stage is over… and he will get nowhere near the level of intimacy and validation that he has grown accustomed to. With the "playboy" skills that he has learned over the years of bedding dozens of women, he could literally pick up his phone and have a for-sure sexual encounter lined up for that evening. Instead, he has a wife who is physically letting herself go, emotionally shutting down, and refusing all physical intimacy.

It's ironic how this type of man tends to marry women who are very low in sexual *"openness,"* a crucial personality trait for remaining intimate and sexual with a partner of many years. What these men see initially as people with stability and good moral compasses end up being the most drab and boring humans in long-term relationships.

Mr. Playboy tends to not last long as a bored married man. Affairs are common. Getting busted is also very common. Divorce is the usual result.

Mr. Playboy is just not marriage material. There's nothing WRONG with that. That's just who he is.

MR. SUPER PROVIDER

On top of our desire to have sex and impregnate as many females as possible, we also have the innate desire to provide for our loved ones, females in particular. We see this played out in the full spectrum of the relationship experience. The boy buys the girl dinner and pays for the movie during their first date, buys her a corsage for their school dance, pays for the engagement ring, brings home the paycheck, etc. Even when the woman in question is a high earner, the male still has a genuine need to step up and provide.

Just like Mr. Playboy and his sexual needs run amok, we can swing the pendulum in the other direction and see another extreme example of taking male needs too far: Mr. Super Provider.

Mr. Super Provider never really has had much luck with girls. Yes, he may have had a *"girlfriend"* in high school for a little while, but it probably ended as soon as they went off to college. The girlfriend probably "didn't want to be tied down" when she went on to the next chapter of her life. In other words, Mr. Super Provider's resources were no longer needed.

The heartbroken Mr. Super Provider moves on to college life where, again, he doesn't have much luck with girls. He does eventually hang out with some girls from his dorm and finds himself doing their homework for them and giving them rides to the mall. None of these "relationships" ended in sexual fun for him. He felt dejected and worthless as a man. His provider qualities never resulted in getting his most basic sexual needs met. The two innate needs, for sex and to provide, never seemed in harmony with each other, but they were both equally strong.

After college, he will meet many different people and make his mark as a good earner. This will result in attention from young women who are looking to "settle down" and find a partner who will be a steady and safe person to go through life with (sound familiar?). Considering Mr. Super Provider's codependent nature and lack of relationship skills, he will attract (and be attracted to) some not-so-good relationship candidates.

Most of the gals that Mr. Super Provider meets will be extremely skilled in the art of taking advantage of needy men. That is, after all, what Mr. Super Provider is. He's needy. He gives and gives. He chases. When that doesn't work, he gives more. What he doesn't realize is that his behavior is a massive turnoff to the more grounded and emotionally stable women in the world. They meet him, get turned off, and go in the other direction. His behavior is, ironically, pushing away the very women that would benefit him the most. On the other hand, the more conniving and dangerous women meet Mr. Super Provider, quickly recognize his neediness, and they do all they can to snag him in their webs of deceit.

Mr. Super Provider is taken advantage of. He's been thrown into a game that he is ill-equipped to handle. He's a little toddler that has wandered out onto the floor during an NBA basketball game. Players are knocking him over, stepping on him, and dunking the ball on his tiny head. He's confused. He was told that he was ready to play the game. He was told that he had what it takes to be a star player, and now everyone is laughing at him.

Mr. Super Provider could very well be a great husband to somebody, but it will take a tremendous amount of work to figure out the source of his codependence, strip him of his neediness, get him to see the full picture, and learn more about the relationship game so that he doesn't keep getting trampled. But, for now, marriage is not for him.

(I cover more of the Lover/Provider dynamic in Chapter 4: The Relationship Game)

THE CHAOS QUEEN

Some women are just dealt a bad hand in life. They endure a childhood that is filled with chaos and uncertainty. They may have had a stable foundation in the early stages of their adolescence, but that was quickly snagged away, and it's been shaky ground ever since. Mom and dad divorced. Mom's negative and possible narcissistic personality traits are amplified. Dad is long gone. The stage is set. The girl known as the Chaos Queen is born.

Many women that come from such a background create chaos in all of their subsequent relationships in life. It's not uncommon for them to be married several times, have kids from multiple men, and have a bevy of unhealthy coping mechanisms to deal with the childhood trauma that they refuse to face. These women are usually paired with Mr. Super Provider types. This type of union never ends well.

The Chaos Queen is ill-equipped to handle the inevitable boredom that comes with a long-term monogamous relationship. She doesn't have the skills to *"spice things up"* or *"keep things fun"* with her spouse. Instead, she looks outside of the relationship for her fix. Her drug is chaos. That's all she has known her whole life, so throwing her into a world of safety and domesticity makes her feel like a hungry tiger in a cage. She'll eventually break free and leave a trail of bloody victims in her wake.

Chaos Queens are not wired for marriage.

MRS. DULL

A woman has parents who have been married for decades. She has several siblings who are also married, and they never divorced. She has no history of any chaos, so to speak. No emotional trauma. No apparent dysfunction. No emotional instability. At the early stages of her relationship with her now husband, she was very loving and sweet. Very sexual. Unbeknownst to the husband, this wasn't the *"real"* her. The real her was what we call *"Mrs. Dull."*

Many guys married to Mrs. Dull will go on and on about how she is perfectly great in all facets of life together, but she just seems to have zero desire to be intimate with her partner. She doesn't like to hold hands. She doesn't like to kiss. She will have sex maybe twice per month (during ovulation), but most of the time that seems to be out of a sense of obligation. She will often be blunt about the nature of the *"pity sex."* She may say things like, *"Hey, it's been a while. We have ten minutes. We can go to the bedroom, if you want."*

When pressed to come up with reasons for his wife's cold nature, the man may start by blaming himself. Maybe she's just not attracted to him. Maybe he can put in more work. The man will improve his physicality, help more around the house, try to be more loving and thoughtful, take his wife out on date nights… but nothing seems to be able to break through this woman's cold exterior. Eventually, the man comes to a realization: This is how everyone in his wife's family behaves. He watches her mom and dad during

Christmas and notices that they never hug. Come to think of it, he's never seen anyone in her family hug and kiss. None of her siblings are loving with their spouses. Nobody holds hands. No back rubs. No leg squeezes. Certainly no butt pinches!

"But, she was very loving when we first got together," the typical husband of Mrs. Dull will say. As I will often reply, *"Yeah, but that was in the honeymoon phase. That's not the real her. That's her in the early stages of love. That's Mother Nature making sure she does all she can to snag a new mate. She's unknowingly becoming the most attractive version of herself. As you can see, she doesn't have that same innate urge once she's married and comfortable. That's just not part of her personality."*

In the good ol' days, this type of cold and unloving relation-ship was not uncommon. Two people got together, and both realized, without actually verbalizing it, that marriage wasn't really for all of that *"lovey dovey"* stuff. Marriage was for making babies, working, and helping each other go through life with minimal trauma. In today's version of marriage, we want our lover, caretaker, co-parent, and best friend all in one package. Mrs. Dull is playing by the old playbook. She thinks she can put all of her eggs in the *"good parent"* basket and that is more than enough to stay with her man until the day she dies. For many men, she is very, very wrong.

Mrs. Dull will have to put in a lot of work and make very real adjustments to her personality in order to succeed as a wife in today's world.

As many men can attest, they may not have a wife as completely shut off and cold as Mrs. Dull, but most of us do notice that our wives' *"sexuality"* knob gets turned down when we marry them… and it gets turned way down after kids come into the picture.

MONOGAMY, AND MARRIAGE IN PARTICULAR, LESSENS A WOMAN'S SEXUAL DESIRE AND OVERALL ZEST FOR LIFE

This probably surprises you. Yes, if you want to increase the chances of your partner getting bored, questioning her life with you, questioning her overall role in the world, detaching from you, and maybe even seeking other sexual partners, then you should marry her and have kids. Allow me to explain.

We all know the tried-and-true trope of the girlfriend who had a wild and crazy sex drive prior to marriage, but she became a cold and timid shrew immediately after saying, *"I do."* A lot of men in this state of marital hell believe that their wives committed a fraudulent *"bait and switch"* on them, trapping them and their resources with the implied promise of fantastic lifelong sex. The theory is that once her man shows his full commitment by taking her hand in marriage, she is then free to relax and show her TRUE asexual colors. *"I'm sorry. Sex is just not that important to me. Most women are like that,"* she will often say.

Is this scenario really that common? Yes. Is it a matter of women just pretending to be crazy about the man until the point of marriage, and then relaxing and ending the charade once the ring goes on their fingers? Well, I'm sure that happens occasionally… but it's not as common as you think. There may be something else going on here.

Familiarity breeds contempt. You've heard that one before, right? It's usually interpreted as: *"When I see you every damn day, you annoy me and eventually I dislike you."* As far as the woman in your life is concerned, it's a little more complex than that. The full story requires that you better understand the interesting but somewhat confounding world of the female mind.

WOMEN WANT WHAT THEY CAN'T HAVE

If the relationship is a comfortable for-sure *"he's not going anywhere no matter what"* kind of relationship… then the process of turning down the female sexual engine begins. For some women (those with hefty personal baggage), the simple act of marriage can shut off the desire for their men instantly. She won the prize, now she doesn't want it anymore. It's that bit of early relationship anxiety and insecurity she used to have that started the process of pushing her *"must have sex with this man"* button. You can think of it as Mother Nature telling her, *"This man must be important and desired by many women if he's not eager to immediately settle down with you. Is he seeing other girls!? If so, he must be a really valuable mate! You should make a baby with him while you have the chance! Lock him down!"*

She needs that excitement. She needs that uncertainty.

She needs that newness and spontaneity. When she locks you down, you become a *"for sure"* thing. You're not going anywhere. That *"I need this man"* button is just not pushed down as much as it used to be. Over time, the button is pushed down less and less… and eventually cobwebs form around it.

Keep in mind that the comfort of marriage can very well turn down sexual desire in the wife… but not necessarily for every man on the planet and for every situation. Her libido is not turned off completely, as most men seem to think. It's just dormant. Women can be horny creatures, but just not often within the confines of marriage. That is a fact many men seem completely blind to, even after watching their wives stare at man butts, read erotic novels (Fifty Shades of Grey made bazillions in book and movie sales), use their vibrators regularly, and listen to them talk to their friends about the cute guy at the office.

She may certainly LOVE her man and want to die old with him, but that certain spark and special something that they had early on… is gone. That upsets her, too.

The grand irony of marriage. Women want to get married. Women want the big wedding. They want the house and 2.5 kids. They want the white picket fence, the dog, and the doting husband that helps with the child-rearing and the housework. They absolutely, positively, genuinely want all of that. It's their lifelong dream. Unfortunately, their primitive sexual engine disagrees. Inside their brains there is a battle going on between their social conditioning, their

need for safety and security, and the DNA that encapsu-
lates hundreds of thousands of years of female reproductive
strategy and instinct all telling them to keep their options
open. Instinct often wins if the environment is right for it to
blossom.

THERE ARE LOTS OF OPPORTUNITIES TO STEP OUTSIDE OF THE MARRIAGE

Let's say you have your typical married woman in the 1950s who honestly wasn't emotionally and sexually fulfilled. Her lustful *"new relationship energy"* with her husband was long gone. She was relegated to a life of kids, kids, housework, and more kids. Her husband most likely propositioned her for sex on a regular basis. She certainly didn't feel like it, but she felt obligated to do it. It was her wifely duty. Besides, if she didn't, her husband may have run off with that cute blond secretary at work! What would people have thought of her if that happened! Everyone would have thought she was a terrible wife! What if he divorced her! The horror!

Now, take that same wife and give her an awesome job, a social circle with at least three or four close friends who recently divorced, a workout class that she joined just last month, a phone constantly buzzing with social media notifications, that cute guy from the office sending her innocent text messages, and endless TV shows depicting the glamorous life of a sexy single woman. Wow, that's a lot of anti-marriage ammunition right there. Couple that environment with a low-boundary woman who never learned how to cope properly with the inevitable dullness of life, and she'll be questioning her marriage faster than you can say, *"I love you but I'm not IN LOVE with you."*

Thanks to the changing marital landscape and the infinite number of communication channels that the internet provides, there are way more opportunities for a wife to see that the *"grass is greener"* wherever she may look.

She hears stories of awesome one-night stands from her divorced friends. Those same friends invite her out for cocktails and dancing, but she can't because of her responsibilities at home. This makes her sad. *"Sigh… must be nice to just be able to go out whenever you want. I have to come home to a mess, kids, and sulking husband."*

She meets a whole new group of people in her CrossFit class. Women who don't seem to have an ounce of fat on their bodies. Young men and women who can do pull-ups and kettle bell swings all day long. Well-muscled men her age who all give her high-fives and tell her that's she's looking good. That one really cute guy who told her she needs to wear those leggings more often while giving her a playful wink. *"Oh man… the things I would do to that guy,"* she says to her divorced friend during wine night. *"Oh my god, you should totally go for it. You only live once,"* her twice-divorced friend says after a few too many drinks.

TEMPTATION IS EVERYWHERE

Don't get me wrong, the world has always been filled with temptation. People have been having extramarital affairs and leaving their partners for generations, but this environment we're in now makes the temptation and avenues for *"stepping over the line"* so much easier to fall victim to. Your wife can literally reach into her pocket and pull out a supercomputer phone that has the capability of instantly talking to dozens of thirsty men all waiting to jump her bones. They can exchange photos, videos, Snap Chat, Instagram, Facebook… there are lots of options at their disposal. Everything that in the old days would be accomplished over the course of a multi-year extended love affair can now be accomplished in one afternoon of texting back and forth. You can go from saying, *"Hi, it's Becky from CrossFit. I just wanted to say hi and thank you for watching my form on those squats yesterday,"* to your wife showing a video of her naked body playing with sex toys… all in the same conversation. It happens.

BAGGAGE

When men tell me about their exes going crazy and leaving them and the kids to go run off with some loser guy with a face tattoo, the first words out of my mouth are usually: *"So, tell me about her mom."* Invariably, I will hear horror stories about their wives' crazy moms who spent years jumping from man to man, had a history of substance abuse, frequently abandoned their kids, often got fired from a list of menial jobs, etc. Mom was a real mess… and she was probably the wife's number one female role model in life. That role model did not provide the sanity and security she needed while growing up. She provided the exact opposite. I've heard this more than a few times: *"It's funny. She always despised everything her mom stood for. Couldn't stand her. Then she became an exact carbon copy of her."*

Popular culture likes to demonize the "deadbeat dad," the guy who walked away from his family and refuses to help provide for the children. Yes, that scenario exists. These stereotypes don't fall from the sky, after all. Men can be awful humans, as we are all well aware of. But what we rarely hear about is the toxic mom. While the absent father may plant seeds of abandonment in the sensitive and malleable child's brain, it's the toxic mom that will further poison them and continuously feed their brains a steady diet of awfulness that will have repercussions for the rest of their lives. In short, was her mom a basket case? Then your wife's capacity for being the same is very high.

Your ex's childhood is a big part of what we call her personal *"baggage."* Baggage is another word for all the negative stuff that happened to her in the past and is now deeply embedded in her psyche and ready to bubble up at a moment's notice. So, when your wife acts crazy and rebellious and has abandoned the kids, she's probably acting out all the psychological baggage in her life that she never properly dealt with. Her mom did crazy stuff when she was a kid. She never properly processed or got help with how to deal with it, and she becomes her mom. Simple. It's textbook behavior.

To further illustrate the concept, picture baggage as a bunch of luggage in the back of a car. A woman who has a shit-ton of baggage is barreling down the road in a car with suitcases and duffle bags poking out of the back windows. The trunk is so full that it can't close. It's stuck open and tied down with bungee cords. It's a mess. The weight of the baggage is so much that it actually throws off the balance of the car. She has to keep her hands on the wheel at all times and constantly make corrections with little tugs left and right. The second she takes her hands off the wheel… SCREEECH! She's off the road and headed for a tree. Disaster.

A person's baggage absolutely will have a negative impact on their life and their relationships with others… unless they recognize the baggage for what it is, live in reality, and take steps towards remedying the situation. Unfortunately, for many women, they have been fed a steady diet of "you are perfect the way you are" and *"you go girl"* throughout their long histories of poor life decisions. She has a growing fan club of friends and family ready to applaud her every step of the way. The thought of being *"damaged"* and needing to do the hard work to improve themselves is pushed aside in favor of living in the moment and in a fog of artificial happiness that everyone seems to glorify.

Now, men, I'm not about to let you off the hook. You have your own baggage you never dealt with, too. I'm just going by the over one thousand guys I've spoken to over the years, and it's safe to say that they all had baggage that helped lead them to the awful situations they found themselves in. They all had childhood issues they never quite dealt with effectively, and it bit them on their asses in the worst way. For most of these guys, they had a series of life events that eventually gave them a severe case of **Nice Guy Syndrome.**

NICE GUY SYNDROME

After reading this book, I whole-heartedly recommend you go out and buy a copy of **No More Mr. Nice Guy** by Dr. Robert Glover. I have recommended that book to thousands of guys over the years, and all who bought it came back to me and said it was the ultimate eye-opener for them. Discovering their codependent *"nice guy"* traits was another enormous piece in the puzzle of figuring out WHY their marriages went down the toilet.

Dr. Glover has done an excellent job of identifying and helping to eliminate a phenomenon that has brought down so many men. I won't go into all the specifics of the book, but the core tenet is that so many of us men have been led to believe that we should be as agreeable as possible and not rock the boat in our interpersonal relationships. In doing so, people in our lives (women in particular) will walk all over us. This makes us bitter and not-so-nice men that live in a world of what we feel SHOULD be rather than what is. We get mad when people we have personal relationships with don't act in the particular way that we expect them to… but we never tell these people exactly what it is we expect of them! This is what Dr. Glover calls a *"covert contract."*

Here's a very real-world example of a covert contract in action:

Your wife tells you she is going out with her friends from work next Friday. They're all celebrating a coworker's birthday. Amongst the group of friends planning to go out is an ex-boyfriend of your wife. Understandably, you don't feel exactly right about it, but you don't feel comfortable telling your wife how you really feel. You don't want to come across as a jealous, controlling husband. After all, your wife SHOULD know better than to go out partying with an ex-boyfriend. You shouldn't HAVE to tell her. Plus, you don't have the energy to deal with the drama that will erupt from you saying NO to her. So, you tell her you don't mind at all and decide to sit back and watch what she does. As planned, she goes out with the friends (and the ex-boyfriend) for a wild night of drinking.

Your wife drunkenly texts you throughout the night. Each text gets a little sillier and more nonsensical. You're trying to read the kids a bedtime story, and she's happily texting things like, *"OMG. Stacey just spilled her drink on Sally's crotch! She looks like she peed her pants!! LOL!"* After a few more of those messages, you are officially beyond annoyed. You are seething and barely able to sleep. She eventually returns home and stumbles into bed after 3:00am.

The next morning, she is badly hung over and not able to help with the kids and their normal Saturday-morning routine. She just lies in bed moaning and saying she feels like she's going to throw up. The more she whines, the angrier you get. You go online and see her social media posts with images from the night before. There are dozens of photos of them hanging out at the bar, getting drunker and drunker as the night goes on. Lots of laughing and dancing. There are exactly twelve photos of her with her ex-boyfriend. They are posing together for the camera, joking around, and making drunken sexual poses with each other. One photo makes it look like he is humping her doggy style while she grabs her friend's boobs… in a fully clothed pseudo threesome. Hilarious. They're laughing and spilling their drinks, having a great time. You're officially livid. THIS is not the behavior of a mom or of a wife. This is completely embarrassing and inappropriate.

You stomp around the house, picking up messes and doing household chores, grunting and loudly sighing with every movement. Your wife finally sits up in bed and asks, *"What's wrong with you?"* That's it. You can't hold back anymore. *"What's wrong with ME?! What's wrong with YOU? What kind of mom goes out drinking and partying with an ex-boy-friend until 3:00am!? Those photos you posted online are fucking embarrassing! You're a married mom of two kids! What is wrong with you?!"* Instead of apologizing, the wife points the finger right back at you. *"I told you what we had planned. I asked you if it was ok. Obviously, you had a real problem with it. Why didn't you just tell me you didn't want me to go? I would've stayed home. I didn't HAVE to go. It was just innocent fun with the old gang from work."* How does every "nice guy" husband respond in this scenario? *"I shouldn't HAVE to tell you!"*

In this example, both the husband and wife have a valid point, but the responsibility for how the whole situation played out ultimately lies at the feet of the husband. He was asked for his opinion up front, and he didn't have the balls to share his true feelings. He chickened out. He didn't want to rock the boat. He didn't want to come across as a controlling asshole. In a roundabout way, he was actually being MORE controlling in the end. He knew exactly how that night would turn out, and he held back his opinion just so he could later have his *"Ah ha! Gotcha!"* moment. He'll never admit it, but it was a passive-aggressive stunt. Most nice guys are experts at passive-aggressiveness and holding back their true feelings in the right moment. For example, the nice guy won't dare tell his wife that she needs to eat better and lose weight. He won't tell his wife when she's acting like a bitch. He won't tell the boss at work that he deserves a raise. He won't tell his friends that he expects them to help him move since he helped them so many times. Instead, he will just sit back, watch the people in his life act against his best interests… and he will be pissed about it. He feels they should all be acting better and more aware of his feelings. The resentment builds and builds until he eventually blows his top or just quietly lives a life of stress and quiet regret.

The nice guy introduces stress and resentment into his life (and subsequently into the lives of those around him) simply because he refuses to play the part of the bad guy for a few measly seconds. The man with the rapidly expanding wife should've sat her down and told her he loves her with all his heart, but looks and health are very important to him, and they should be important to her, too. Starting tomorrow, they will start working out together so she can lose weight and be a woman he is attracted to and be a good healthy role model for the kids. The man being pushed around at work and being passed over for a promotion should tell his boss that he has worked his butt off for so many years and brings a lot to the company, and therefore deserves a raise. The man with the asshole friends should tell them he has always been there for them when they needed him the most and he expects them to drop what they're doing every now and then to help when he needs them, too. These are things that men with a strong sense of self-worth do. This is a mentally- healthy approach to life and conflict.

The commonality among these honest-dude moments is the recognition that he is taking a risk by standing up for himself. He's more than willing to take the loss if he has to. The husband is willing to divorce a lazy, overweight wife who just doesn't care anymore, the employee is polishing his resume and ready to resign at any moment, and the annoyed guy is willing to tell his deadbeat friends to fuck off. In other words, a strong man realizes that he needs to stand up for himself and his principles, but he knows it may very well bite him in the ass. He's prepared for it. The honest man knows that if he just tries to smooth things over and be the nice guy all the time, it will just make matters worse. Being nice all the time is just a form of denial.

Being nice is also another way of saying that you are being a very agreeable person. Agreeableness is one of the big five personality traits that is higher in women. When you just go with the flow and don't put your foot down and stick up for yourself, you're being more effeminate, less manly, and therefore more unattractive to women.

STRESS

There's healthy early relationship anxiety, and then there's the stress and pressure of real, everyday married life. The stress and insecurity of everyday life absolutely kill a woman's sexual desire. The further you remove her from the fantasy world of the lustful beginnings of the hot and heavy relationship, the more her sexual desire and overall zest for life decreases.

While her sexual desire can go into dormancy, there is a very basic truth underneath: Your wife has normal human needs and they're not being met. In fact, the stress of life makes her NEED for excitement and escape from her life grow exponentially. This is why, by my estimation, one of the most affair-prone people in a relationship is the professional working mom who has way too much on her plate. With the constant state of stress and anxiety, coupled with the aforementioned opportunities to cross the line, and the apparent lack of constraints around the marriage, it doesn't take much for her to act in a not-so-good way.

Let me illustrate further the difference between men and women and the relationship between sexual desire and stress. Think about a really shitty and stressful day at work. Your boss calls you into his office to let you know that the company will make some cuts to the staff, and he may have to let you go. It's not 100% sure yet. He's trying to convince the big bosses to keep you and your team on the job, but it's not looking good. He wanted to let you know so that you can prepare in case he has let you all go. Now you're in an ultra-stressed state of employment limbo. *"Will I get fired? Do I get a paycheck next month? What will my wife think?"*

If after this news you went home and told your wife all the horrible details of your day and she said, *"Alright… you know what you need, mister? You need a blowjob,"* you would be all for it. No questions asked. Hallelujah. A blowjob is absolutely the best medicine at that moment. Your "ready for sex" button is always on at the edge of being fully pressed down, and hearing *"Blowjob?"* pushes it the rest of the way. At that moment, you feel like you have the best wife on the planet Earth. She just validated you and your worth as a man.

Let's look at this scenario in a much more realistic way. The husband comes home and says to the wife, *"We need to talk."* He then dumps on her all of this horrible news about the meeting with his boss and his job possibly going away. Instantly, the wife thinks about bills not being paid, the lights getting turned off, not being able to care for the kids properly, not buying stuff she wants when she wants, her friends finding out that her husband is unemployed… it's all too much to bear.

Sex with her husband? A blowjob? What about it? Uh, no thank you. Her sexual desire is now completely gone. Sex with her husband is not even an option when life dumps such a stressful load of shit in her lap. Her cavewoman brain just said to her, *"The Provider male can no longer care for you and the family. He can't protect you. Shut down the sexual engine immediately. You don't want to have a baby with this horrible financial situation hanging over your head. This male is a suboptimal life mate."* In a relatively short time, her body and brain may very well say, *"Time to look at alternative mates that can better provide for us."* It's not evil, as some would contend. It's human nature.

"So, let me get this straight," men all say. *"She's turned off by the comfort and familiarity of married life, and she's turned off when shit hits the fan and life gets stressful for her? Both comfort and stress within the marriage cause her to shut down sexually?"* Yes, exactly. *"So, we can't win."* No, you can, but most men don't have the relationship skills (or the right partner) needed to acquire and KEEP a loyal wife through all of life's hard times. It's tremendously hard to maintain a long-lasting sexual relationship with a woman in today's social climate.

PUTTING WOMEN ON A PEDESTAL

A man notices that his wife has been acting strangely over the past couple of months. She's been putting in way more hours at work. She's been going out regularly with her friends. She has been dressing sexier and lost a lot of weight. She's been on her phone non-stop. She will often bicker and snap at her husband for no apparent reason, trying to start fights on a daily basis. He saw her texting somebody and then deleting the texts when he walked by. Weird.

The husband is talking to a friend over beers and he brings up his wife's strange behavior. His friend listens and grows more concerned with every detail of the story. Finally, his friend stops him and says, *"Wait. Dude. Come on. Seriously? She's totally cheating on you."* Husband is taken aback by this accusation. *"What?! No, dude. She's not like that. She's very much against cheating. Always has been. It's gotta be some-thing else."*

Men just love to put their women up on the pedestal of moral perfection. Even with mounting evidence of wrong-doing, a man will often be in complete denial, unable to see what is so obvious to everyone around him. *"Nope, not my wife. No way."* Even after discovering that she is lying to him, he will quickly let that slide. *"Okay, she lied about THAT... but she would never do that OTHER thing."* He keeps moving the goalposts. He keeps changing the rules so that she never wins the coveted trophy that says, *"She's just a broken, awful human being after all.*" To nice guys with no boundaries and a fear of conflict (and the possibility of abandonment), there is no choice but to put the woman at a higher moral level than him. She is the beacon of hope in a world filled with dread and anxiety. If that crumbles, what does he have left to lean on?

Why is it so common for men to put women on a pedestal? What is going on in the mind of a man that he would elevate a normal human to superhuman levels… just because of their gender? Well, like with most things in life, it starts when we are young. For a lot of men, a combination of puberty and childhood anxiety caused girls to be highly desirable, but frustratingly off-limits. The boys' own fears, sexual shame and low self-image put up unnatural barriers between themselves and girls. For high-anxiety, low self-esteem boys, there is nothing as terrifying as asking a girl out and possibly being rejected.

As we mature and become horny out-of-control late teen boys, the pedestalization gets further amplified. We are torn between feelings of romance/love and unbridled testosterone-fueled horniness. We dream of walking hand-in-hand with Ms. Perfect, talking on the phone for hours, going to the movies… and also fantasize about banging her in the basement on the washing machine while the parents are gone. During the spin cycle, of course. Our shameful male sexuality is at odds with our need for female companionship. We've been told again and again to subdue our sexuality and to prop up our sweet and thoughtful behaviors instead. Being a *"gentleman,"* we are told, is key for *"winning"* the hand of a good girl. The common lingo of terms like *"winning"* and *"getting lucky"* are examples of social norms that elevate the woman to superhuman levels and further shame the male for his natural inclinations. This starts very young for all men.

After years of nice guy behavior and pedestalization of women in his life, the typical nice guy has an elaborate fantasy life where all the pretty girls in his social circle suddenly realize just how nice and perfect he is. No longer does he have to watch the good-looking jocks and confident assholes date the prettiest and sweetest girls in class. His sex life will then reach levels of awesome depravity only seen in the pornography he has become addicted to. Obviously, this is a fantasy that never pans out. He may say he's too much of a gentleman, not a dumb jock, too smart, or too kind, but the truth is that he's just too scared to make the obvious changes needed to become successful with women.

After finally landing a woman (usually she has to approach him or friends push him to her), the nice guy latches on like a tick and will not let go, no matter what happens. This inevitably results in a man who gladly overlooks many red flags under the guise of being a sensitive and understanding partner. The entirety of his being is centered on the relationship with his woman. He has no choice but to overlook red flags. Without her and their relationship, he has nothing of real substance in his life. Everyone else in his social circle probably takes advantage of him, so to come home to *"unconditional"* love from his perfect wife is an oasis in the desert of life's awfulness. To suddenly tell him that the oasis was really a mirage all along is traumatizing. *"Nope. She would never do that. She's not like that."*

Putting women on a pedestal is also a subtle form of sexism. Women are often looked at as timid, overly kind, weak little pixies of love and romance. They need to be handled gently or else they will spaz out uncontrollably in fits of emotion. As a result, many people think we can't involve women in such rational or tough-minded things, such as running a business or playing a sport. We also can't involve them in our perverse male-centered world of our sexuality. They're women. They're way different. They're actually BETTER, in many ways, we tell ourselves. They belong up on the pedestal looking down on us sport-playing, porn-loving, penis-having ingrates.

It's all bullshit, of course. Not only is it demeaning to paint women with such a wide behavioral brush, but it's only setting men up for severe future relationship failure. A man sees the woman as a delicate creature worthy of praise and optimism… when he should treat her with the same level of rational skepticism he applies to the men in his life. She's a human being. She can be an evil, sex-loving, business-running, violent asshole, too.

Not only is putting women on a pedestal unrealistic and unfair, it is also a potent female libido killer. SHE wants to look up to HIM, not look down on him. If you put her up on the highest of pedestals, she has no choice but to look down on you… and thus lose respect for you. She may say she wants to be treated like a princess, but only if her man is the king. The nerd who brings flowers to the prom queen and professes his love will get turned down around 100% of the time. The tall handsome jock with a natural charm who hands the prom queen a half-eaten piece of beef jerky and says, *"Yer kinda hot, I guess,"* will get laughs and lots of sex in the not-too-distant future.

SHE LOST RESPECT FOR YOU

Simply put, respect is everything to a woman. As soon as she deems you unworthy of her respect, she will immediately have her eyes open and scanning for Mr. Replacement (this may or may not be a conscious decision on her part). Do you know how many times I've heard from men that have been dumped by their partner, *"Well, my wife got a promotion at work and she started making a lot more than me,"* or, *"I was laid off from work and couldn't find a job for three months, but that was okay because her job was more than enough to pay the bills for a while"*? It is very common. For some women, the mere idea of their men making less money than them is enough to start the process of emotional detachment. Yes, it's stupid and shallow, but it's certainly not unheard of.

This need for respect is so strong, that sometimes money isn't the issue, but the PERCEPTION of money and status is. For example, I had a guy contact me who made way more money than his wife. She worked at a big corporation in some management job, sitting at a cubicle making five figures a year doing cost-saving projects. He, on the other hand, made six figures by working several productive jobs at once. He owned and managed several rental properties, ran a small landscaping company with his brother, and sold collectibles on eBay. It wasn't a *"traditional"* one paycheck job, but it was honest work, gave his family plenty of money, and…. he was happy! The wife, though… she was obviously not too impressed. Towards the end of their marriage, she kept making comments about positions opening up in her company and pressuring him to submit his resume.

Him: *"Why would I stop what I'm doing now to go work in an office and make just $60k like you? I make way more than that."*

Her: *"Well, you'd have more job security, for one thing."*

Him: *"Your company just laid off a bunch of people last year. Remember how you were all stressed about it? How is that more security?"*

Her: *"Well, I just don't think you should shut out opportunities like this. A lot of people would kill for a job there."*

This topic started coming up ALL the time. He finally figured out what the real problem was. He noticed when they were at company gatherings or meeting people for the first time, his wife would get really weird when people asked him what he did for a living. She always tried to change the topic or walked away from the conversation. He eventually asked her about it, and she admitted that, yes, it was kind of embarrassing to hear him tell people he was a landlord, landscaper, and an eBay seller. Other husbands in their group had normal jobs like dentist or sales manager. It made him sound like a loser in comparison. She didn't want to be seen as the wife of a loser.

He was completely insulted and shocked by her admission. The woman he loved, the mother of his children, his best friend, was telling him this shallow nonsense. Did she forget he brought home way more money than she did?! Did she forget all the things he had paid for over the years? Also, he was no dummy. He was an educated man. He was intelligent. He was hard-working. He busted his butt every single day for the family… and he was extremely happy while doing it. To him, that was a win-win. To his wife, all that mattered was that his perceived value was possibly low compared to other men. She was afraid of what her social group may have thought.

This lack of respect was eventually the straw that broke the camel's back, and it wasn't long before she finally filed for divorce. She did so after jumping on a man with a suitable job title and social cachet. It's common knowledge that women rarely leave a relationship without having another one standing by.

Admittedly, his lack of a *"good enough"* job title wasn't THE thing that ruined their marriage. In hindsight, his marriage troubles began shortly after his wife had their third kid. He saw numerous red flags that showed she wasn't coping well with the changing relationship dynamics and the stress that came with being a working parent of three. Her pressuring him to take on a different job was just a last-ditch effort to keep the marital machine running. *"Please, at least change your job so I can have some respect for you and possibly stop these repeated feelings I have about leaving you."*

This one stings for a lot of guys because it cuts to the heart

of the matter and exposes the ugly side of their relationships. It shows that their wives' love for them does in fact
have conditions, and one condition may be as simple and
stupid as *"Have a job title that impresses my social group."*
The good husband was proud to say he stuck with his wife
through thick and thin, loved her for her mind and her
heart, overlooked things like her weight gain and often
bitchy attitude, was proud to call her his wife… but she
looked for a replacement because his job title or paycheck
was not that impressive?! Yes. It happens.

OTHER WOMEN LOST INTEREST IN YOU, AND YOU LOST INTEREST IN OTHER WOMEN

This one is a real head-scratcher for a lot of guys. Many wives will punish and shame their husbands if they look at or make any kind of sexual reference to other women. The husband says, *"Oh, she's cute,"* and the wife immediately stops what she's doing and scowls. *"Cute!? How can you think that's a good thing to say? She's like twenty years old. Do you like teen girls, too? What about your daughter's friends? You should really think before you say stuff like that, because it's creepy and hurtful to me."* Ouch. Husband goes back to his man cave with his tail between his legs. The message is clear: No other girls are attractive. Ever. Only his wife. To think otherwise is sacrilege.

The wife's shaming of her husband's sexuality is an extremely common scenario. It's an understood cultural norm. This is why men always hide their porn, sneak away to strip clubs with their buddies, and look straight down at their shoes when that curvy brunette walks by them in the mall. Even the most basic and innocent of actions can set off the wife, and most men can't deal with the stress of a hostile woman. Men just want peace and quiet.

The irony (and there's a lot of irony in relationships, as you'll learn) is that much of this *"flirty"* or *"eye wandering"* behavior that wives shame their husbands for is a crucial piece to unlocking the combination to the wife's sexual desire. Simply put, a man that has sexual options in life is a total turn-on (if you're five hundred pounds and unemployed, this does not pertain to you). If your woman can drop you off at any random bar on a Friday night and never has to worry about women coming on to you, then you are NOT a turn-on. You are a comfortable life partner. You are a for-sure thing. **Remember, comfort and boredom kill female sexual desire.** There needs to be that little bit of uncertainty to keep the flame going. It's one thing to be a good, faithful husband. It's another thing to be a neutered man shamed into pretending to not have urges that every other man on the planet has… just so you don't piss off your wife.

For a married woman, one of the absolute biggest turn-ons is to go to a social event with her man and watch other people, especially women, admire him. If a pretty woman goes up to her man and chats and makes flirty eyes at him, that's a man that is going home that night and getting laid by his wife. Her man went from normal everyday husband to the guy that other high-value women find attractive. His sexual ranking just went through the roof in one night… and all he did was stand there and be himself. He put in zero work, and Mother Nature rewarded him with random female attention. That's a man that stands above the crowd. That's a man who has a wife who says, *"I'm really, really lucky to have a man like THAT."*

SHE BECAME YOUR MOTHER

Parenthood and sexual desire do not work in tandem; they work against each other. Being a parent is the antithesis of being a sexual human being. When your wife is in mom mode, she's only in mom mode. When the baby is screaming, the twelve-year-old is saying he's hungry again, the dog just knocked over his water bowl, and she has a washer full of mildewy laundry she forgot to put in the dryer the night before… the last thing she wants is for her needy/horny husband to come behind her and poke her in the butt with his erection. He may see it as a sexy joke, but his wife sees it as a show of disrespect and lack of awareness of the awful situation spinning around in her brain. The husband might as well take a giant shit on her head. Same result. It just adds to the chaos.

If you REALLY want to take your wife out of the sexy headspace, then become her adult child. Become completely dependent upon her for your day-to-day living. Add to the chaos of her life. Become part of the problem and not a solution. Make sure that she is the only one to organize and make things happen in the family. She makes your dentist appointments, she tells you what clothes to wear to special events, she tells you when you're going out to see your couple friends, she cleans up after you, she feeds you, etc. All of this is not a good recipe for respect and sexual desire. You're just another mouth to feed. Another butt to wipe. You're a helpless creature. Respect goes right out the window with such behavior. She desperately NEEDS you to occasionally take charge and show her your independence. Show her you can absolutely, positively be a happy and productive person if you had to live on your own. A woman that rolls her eyes and laughs at the thought of her helpless husband living on his own is a woman who wants nothing to do with him sexually. *"Oh, God. I can't imagine Robert on his own. He would probably die of starvation or drown in dirty laundry. He's helpless."*

Now, this doesn't mean that running around and doing chores gets your wife turned on and ready for sex and happily committed to you for life. You don't do household chores to win the favor of your wife and *"get lucky"* (that's called *"choreplay"*). You do these things because you're an adult and they need to get done. Whatever you do, don't you dare do the dishes and then sulk when she doesn't want to give you a blowjob that night. Children run to mommy to show her they cleaned up messes and hope for hugs and a *"GOOD JOB!!"* You never want to say, *"Honey, I washed the dishes and did laundry!"* Oh, wow. What do you want, a cookie? No, you want love and affection from your wife. It's obvious, and it's a complete turnoff.

SHE'S JUST CRAZY

As you can see, when trying to piece together the giant puzzle of WHY you find yourself in your current hellish predicament, it can get a little complicated and downright philosophical. We can pontificate about everything from the current state of marriage to the feminization of men. But, sometimes, the simplest answer to it all is the right one.

Sometimes… she's just crazy.

I've had men go on and on for nearly an hour, telling me about all the terrible stuff they have endured from their wives. At one point in a story, the man will nonchalantly mention some piece of information that makes my eyebrows go up. I usually interrupt him with a loud, *"Wait, wait… back up a moment. She did what again?"* One gentleman I spoke to recently mentioned that his wife would punch herself, cut her arms, and run purposely into traffic if he ever put up a boundary of any kind. He casually mentioned this as if he was talking about the weather. I stopped him and said, *"Whoa. Dude. That's pretty bad. She's not well. She needs help beyond anything you can give her."* The man chuckled and said, *"Yeah, that's what everyone else tells me, too."*

Men are put in a tough spot when it comes to dealing with troubled women. We have an innate need to FIX any broken thing we see, to protect our loved ones, and to give the females in our lives a long behavioral leash because, *"Hey… she's a woman. They're all crazy, am I right?"* It's not-so-subtle sexism, but also a false macho front that hides a guy who is secretly too afraid to rock the boat and put up boundaries with his spouse. She's throwing plates at his head and leaving bruises on his face, and he's smiling and shrugging his shoulders. *"Hey, what can you do?"*

What CAN you do, in these cases? For many men, they have learned that pushing away a troubled wife increases the drama exponentially. In the case of the aforementioned client, when he tells his spouse that she shouldn't talk to him that way, she instantly hurts herself. She shows him, with explicit physical self-harm, just how much his words hurt her. The messages are received: *"If it wasn't for you, I wouldn't be doing this to myself. All you have to do is be a good boy, and I won't be in pain."* This appeals to the broken little boy that he has inside of him (from his own past childhood trauma) as well as his innate need to protect his woman and fix her problems. All he has to do is shut the hell up and all will be better.

Sometimes, the troubled wife will see that she has been painted into a corner and is in a losing battle. She can see the switch flip in his eyes and recognizes that he will not take her abuse any longer. He has officially checked out. Like any cornered animal, she lashes out, but not physically. It's not unheard of for a man to find police at his door asking him to get out of the house. His wife, they tell him, filed a complaint and feels unsafe. She worries about her wellbeing and that of the children. *"What does that have to do with me?"* the man will ask. *"I've never touched her or threatened her in my life."* The police don't listen. They are just doing their job. *"Can you pack some things please, sir? Do you have some place you can go tonight?"* Thus begins the process of the broken wife using the justice system as a tool to further abuse her partner. *"If he wants to pull away from me, then this is what he deserves,"* she will tell herself.

As I say to men in these situations, *"She's not well. She needs help. It's not her fault. It's not your fault. She had some pretty shitty stuff happen to her as a kid, and now you and everyone else are paying for it. I'm sorry, but your only course of action is to get the hell outta dodge and try to take your kids with you. Get the law involved. Call for help. She needs to be committed today."*

As Dr. Jordan Peterson once said in an interview with Camille Paglia, *"I don't think that men can control crazy women. There's no step forward that a man can take to win in those circumstances."* Dr. Peterson went on to say that men have an underlying understanding between each other: *"This interaction could get physical… so let's behave and be cordial to each other."* With men and women, it's understood that the man shouldn't even consider raising a hand to a woman, so the interaction becomes solely verbal and emotional. When dealing emotionally with a person who is not mentally well, you're not operating on even ground. The deck is very much stacked against you. You are the rational person in the interaction. How can you possibly gain the upper hand when the other person continuously bends and shifts reality to be in their favor?

BORDERLINE PERSONALITY DISORDER

There is a particular circumstance in the life of women that seems to the lay the groundwork for emotional instability and future relationship trouble: abandonment by a parent. This could be dad leaving, mom leaving, mom and dad divorcing, etc. The commonality in these situations is that the child perceived a life of love and security, and it was suddenly yanked away from them. Their little malleable brains aren't wired to deal with the trauma of living in an uncertain world with a missing parental figure. We know now that the number one predictor of borderline personality disorder (BPD) in women is abandonment. Mom or dad left her when she was young, and she's *"acting out"* this trauma on all of her subsequent relationship partners for the rest of her life. Some men like to call it severe *"daddy issues."* Whatever you want to call it, it's yet another example of our predictable human behavior.

BPD is the extreme form of *"broken woman"* that is unfortunately becoming more and more common. Take a woman from a broken home who has never been taught coping skills or boundaries of any kind, and you have a good chance that she develops full-blown BPD or other personality disorders.

Here are some common BPD behaviors. See if these ring any bells.

1. Love bombing

When that initial infatuation/falling in love/*"I must procreate with this man"* stage hits, it hits the BPD woman hard. Really hard. She will do anything and everything to be with her new man. She will shower him with praise. She will buy him things. She will submit to any and all sexual needs the man may have. She will lose weight. She will dress seductively. She will text or call incessantly. The sex will be amazing. For a man with little dating experience and/or feelings of low self-esteem, this is absolutely the most amazing feeling he has ever experienced. This HAS to mean she is *"the one"* for him, right?!

"I just knew she was the one from the first day we met."

I've heard this more than a few times from my readers who have BPD wives. The worshipping of the BPD partner by the low self-worth man starts right away.

Let's be honest. All men want a woman who love bombs them. To be worshipped and adored at such an extreme level is our dream. Oh, to be king for a day! When we are in the midst of experiencing an extreme BPD love bomb, what should be obvious warning signs of way-too-early and extreme attachment are drowned out by all the fantastic positive emotions we men feel (and the fantastic porn sex, of course).

"When wearing rose-colored glasses, all the red flags just look like flags."

2. Extreme Jealousy

The BPD woman is extremely threatened by the emotional connections you make with others. This could be your attachment to your children, your coworkers, your platonic friends, your ex-girlfriends, etc. She will do all she can to separate you physically and emotionally from these people. In her mind, she must eliminate all competition for her attention.

Her brain, *"Stop all these other relationships! He's going to leave you!"*

3. Morphing

Thanks to their heightened sense of empathy, women are naturally more agreeable and pliable than men. We all know the woman who takes on the personality traits, hobbies, and interests of her new boyfriend. She didn't use to like football, now suddenly she's wearing a Bengals jersey and yelling at the TV during Monday Night Football.

The BPD woman takes this to the next level. She doesn't have that filter or boundary mechanism that says, *"Oh, I like you and all... but I'm not doing THAT. I have self-respect."* Instead, she will gladly put on the football jersey, snort the cocaine, pop the pills, get the tattoo, get the boob job, join the orgy, and ignore her kids for weeks at a time. This is all to keep the new man around and avoid the abandonment she fears more than anything.

4. Splitting

What was once the best thing in the entire universe is now the equivalent of dog shit on the bottom of her shoe. This sudden change in thought, or *"splitting,"* can seem to happen suddenly with no warning. Then, the dog shit goes back to being fantastic again… but only briefly. Then it's back to being awful again.

Usually, that piece of dog shit is the unsuspecting male partner in her life. The husband or boyfriend she was once infatuated with becomes a laughable loser when she meets and bonds with a new man.

Again, this is common cheating woman behavior. Where the BPD woman takes it a step further is that she goes WAY BEYOND indifference towards her ex, and has to destroy him. She will reach out to her social circle to ruin his name. She may try to physically harm him or get others to do it. She may take all his money. She will randomly send him messages, reminding him of just how worthless he is. She will tell the kids how awful he is. She will outright lie about him to anyone he cares about.

She won't stop until he is completely destroyed.

She's getting back at him for *"abandoning"* her. It doesn't matter that SHE cheated, broke up with him, and attached to another man. In her reptilian brain, her ex abandoned her. He failed to play the role she needed. He must pay the price.

There is no grey area with a BPD woman. It's all or nothing. You're either the second coming of Jesus or the
Devil himself.

The *"Oh wow, this is really fucked up"* moment comes when the man finally gets wise and stops all contact with the BPD woman. That is when she is left with her acute fear of abandonment. This is when she will lash out in more anger, sadness, and maybe even self-harm or attempted suicide. This draws the ex back in (as Mr. Codependent Fixer)… and then the cycle continues.

5. Gaslighting

This is a term used when abusive people try to convince you that the red flags you are seeing are actually YOUR fault. YOU are the crazy/mean/cruel/abusive one. She's the victim.

With the BPD woman, it is never her fault. It never will be her fault. She can't see the rational side of things because she is incapable of doing so.

This just makes the *"nice guy"* husband want to try even harder. After all, he made vows to his woman. For better or for worse. Maybe she has a point. That one time, he said she was acting like a bitch. He shouldn't have done that. *"I can be a better husband,"* he tells himself.

She sees his groveling and his attempts to fix the situation, and she grows angrier and more resentful.

This form of abuse has lasting repercussions for the man and his subsequent relationships moving forward in life. He questions everything about himself, and his already low self-esteem is completely flushed down the toilet.

"Maybe I AM the problem. Maybe I AM worthless."

6. Infidelity

In broad terms, BPD women feel two things:

• An intense need for love and acceptance.

• A need to engage in impulsive and risky behavior to illicit a feeling of being *"alive."*

Cheating fits in perfectly with their psyches.

You, the nice/normal guy with low self-esteem, will never be enough for the BPD woman. NOBODY will be enough for her. This is the ultimate irony of BPD. She is frightened to the core about the chance of abandonment by her partner, but she does everything in her power to drive him away… including abuse and actually running into the arms of another man (or multiple men). A BPD woman will often rationalize her frequent infidelities by saying, *"Hey, we all know you were going to cheat on me, anyway."*

Yes, *"normal"* women cheat all the time. The BPD difference is that they often like to rub it in the ex's face.

There are stories of women sending photos of them engaging in sex with their new men, sharing graphic details, explaining how the new partner is physically better/more endowed, etc. This is just part of the *"must punish the old partner for not doing what he was supposed   to"* pathology. Whatever she can do to chip away at the confidence and happiness of the ex-partner, she will do.

JIM'S STORY

Jim was a very successful businessman in charge of a large, multi-generation, family-owned business. He was extremely hard-working and wanted nothing more than to find a wife and start a family. In his early twenties, he met Mary. Mary was very loving and sexual early in their relationship. The courtship process lasted years before they agreed to tie the knot. Soon after, they had two boys. It was soon after her second child that they discovered Mary's serious health issues that would require extensive life-threatening surgery.

Thankfully, Mary made it out of her surgery just fine, but that left her with an unwavering desire to get in tip-top physical shape and do all she could to make sure her body machine was operating properly for years to come. She had stared death in the face, and that gave her the spark she needed to be her absolute best. This is when her fitness obsession began.

Mary soon discovered that she had a gift for bodybuilding. Her physique really blossomed from hours of resistance training, and she ended up looking like a comic book super-hero, complete with chiseled abs and an overall shape that made everyone say, *"Whoa."* But, she wasn't an overly muscled steroid-taking freaky bodybuilder. She still retained her femininity while projecting an image of strength and extreme levels of fitness.

Mary was now hot. Very hot.

This new body garnered a lot of attention online from the various social media sites that she repeatedly posted to. She became somewhat of a quasi-celebrity in the "fitness mom" industry, showing thousands of women all over the world what was possible after giving birth to two kids and surviving a life-threatening condition.

Jim eventually noticed that Mary's new interest went beyond *"healthy hobby"* status and into full-blown obsession. She spent an entire family vacation running from spot to spot, complaining that she could not get a signal on her phone. She needed to post to social media. Her followers were counting on her! That, combined with several dozen other red flags, showed Jim that something wasn't quite right with Mary. He investigated further.

One fateful day, Mary left her cellphone unattended. That's when Jim saw the messages between Mary and another man. Jim was heartbroken by what he saw. Like every other man that endures this type of unwanted surprise, Jim didn't stop with what he saw on the phone. He had to dig further for the real truth. What he saw wasn't pretty.

It turns out that Mary wasn't just in an affair but living secretly as a sexual plaything for a married couple from her gym. The husband and wife worked in tandem to convince Mary to help them act out their porno threesome fantasies. Their sexual dreams eventually came true. Whether Mary was a wife and a mom of two kids didn't seem to matter to Mary or to the horny couple. Like many people in similar situations, the pleasure of the moment trumped any long-term consequences that may have lay ahead.

It took several years and many hundreds of thousands of dollars before Jim and Mary finally agreed on a settlement for the divorce. Mary has since lost any relationship with her children, is no longer involved with the horny gym couple, and has bounced from man to man over the past several years. With hindsight, Jim admits he overlooked many red flags during his marriage to Mary. He said what many guys in his shoes say, *"She ended up being exactly like who she despised the most: her mom."*

CHAPTER 3
WHAT YOU CAN EXPECT MOVING FORWARD

WHY IS SHE ACTING THIS WAY?

When I talk to freshly divorced or separated men, our first session usually consists of the man taking up 90% of the time. He will talk at a rapid-fire pace about one thing and one thing only: The crazy shit that his ex is doing.

"Look, I gave her everything she wanted. She got the house. She gets the alimony she asked for. She still makes little snotty comments about me keeping the Mustang. She says I took advantage of her. Why does it piss her off?! Am I supposed to not have a car?! Do I need to walk to work to make her happy?"

The man is seeing things from a very rational, business-like perspective. He sat down at the negotiating table with the other party. They agreed to the terms of a deal. They shook hands. Now the other party is going on a strange campaign of anger and resentment. It's like they're putting up billboards around town saying, *"I was robbed! This man sucks! Don't trust him!"*

"She was the one that wanted the divorce! She was the one that hired the fancy lawyer and tried to take me to court! I gave her what she wanted! Why am I made out to be the damn villain here?!"

This example is not at all uncommon. Many of you are probably reading this and smiling while saying, *"I see you've met my ex-wife."* This example is a pretty tame one, to be honest. The irrational behavior of a lot of ex-wives can go into *"pretty damn crazy"* territory. Some examples I have heard over the years:

"She cheated on me and divorced me. Three months later, I met a gal and had her over to my house to spend the night. My ex saw the girl's car in the driveway and slashed her tires."

"My ex saw me and my new girlfriend walking around town. She went on a Facebook campaign telling the world what a lying cheater I was during our marriage. I met this new girl four months after our divorce. My ex cheated on ME… not the other way around."

"Towards the end of our marriage, my ex just kept pushing me away. Nothing I did was good. She kept bringing up divorce. I finally relented and agreed. After that, she's been on a scorched-earth campaign to make my life hell."

"My ex and I were amicable as we went through the divorce. Then she found out that I talked to a mutual friend about our situation, and she went ballistic. Her lawyer is now asking for a lot more than we agreed to."

The common theme in these situations is a man who cannot understand what he sees as completely irrational behavior. It's like he's holding up a flash card that reads: "2+2 = 4," and the ex-wife is screaming that the answer is actually five. He keeps looking at the card. *"Uh… no… the answer is four. Always has been four."* The ex-wife just gets more infuriated. *"THE ANSWER IS FIVE! WHY ARE YOU BEING LIKE*

THIS!?"

The answer I give to men in these situations is this: You and
I can't fathom the storm of crazy going on in their heads
right now. For you guys that have discovered your wives'
infidelity and have been subsequently dumped, you're in for
some REAL head-scratching crazy. One day she will act like
a single twenty-something girl ready for her new life, the
next she is back to acting like the domestic forty-four-year-
old mom of three who never even conceived of divorce. This
back and forth will make your head spin. It will, literally,
drive you crazy.

After I discovered my ex's affair and we went through the
one marriage counseling session (that was ridiculously
bad), my ex declared that we were over, and we needed to
stop the charade. She was going to look for another place,
and then we could tell the kids that she was leaving. To say
I was crushed and confused would be an understatement. I
was emotionally destroyed. Coming home after work every
day was a true test of my fortitude. I would come home to
the wife and kids, and the wife would quickly leave and go
elsewhere for the night. I would be mostly ignored, and my
ex would make a show of having to *"go to the gym"* or *"go
do something for work,"* all to put the kids at ease. The kids
never suspected anything was up. I would then feed the
kids, put them to bed, and she would be back early in the
morning before they woke up to take them to school. It was
a strange state of marital limbo and a good test run of my
new divorced life for the next decade.

On one particularly strange day, I came home from work to see that the weeds in the landscaping at the front house had been pulled. This was a project that was long overdue, so it was nice to see that it was done, and I didn't have to worry about it. I walk in the house, and I see my ex sitting on the couch folding laundry. A strange domestic duty for Ms. Midlife Crisis. She looks up at me and smiles and says, *"Hi babe!"* Whoa… what was going on? I just smiled back and said, *"Did you pull the weeds out front?"* She smiled and said, *"Yep!"* I replied, *"Oh… that's awesome. Thank you!"*

As the emotionally crushed guy who was just cheated on and dumped, to see this action from my wife filled me with all kinds of confusion and hope. *"She called me 'babe'… does that mean we're back on as a couple? Why is she acting so nice? Is this her way of apologizing and trying to make amends? What the hell do I do now?"* Later, after dinner, my questions would be answered. She made her usual show of having to go to the gym and didn't return that night. The next day, she was back to her cold, new self.

I can try to rationalize and understand that situation. Maybe she was conflicted and consciously tried to play her old part of wife and mom… but putting that old suit on again felt extremely uncomfortable, so she ran away. Maybe it wasn't even a conscious thing at all. Maybe she just had a complete brain fart, and she went into automated-behavior mode, acting out what she had been doing for the past twenty years with no thought or reason behind it. Then maybe she snapped out of it and realized, *"Wait… what am I doing? I hate this guy now. I have a new guy. Girl, run away!"*

Who knows? Trying to figure this stuff out will just drive
you crazy. I have seen it LITERALLY drive men nuts. Men
lose their sense of reality the more they intertwine with and
try to understand the minds of their exes in these moments.
Eventually, you do what we all do. You just smirk and laugh
it off. You conclude that it's just part of who she is now.
There's nothing to comprehend or understand. She's just
moving in whatever direction her emotional wind takes her.
Just try to stand out of the way so that you don't get hurt.

WHAT OTHERS THINK IS VERY IMPORTANT TO HER

Shortly after the infamous weed-pulling incident, my ex
found her own place to live. A friend of a friend had a cheap
house for her to rent. Thus began the process of telling the
kids (the worst experience of my life) and my ex slowly
moving things out of the house. I would come home from
work each day, and a few more items of hers would be gone.
It was done quietly and with relatively little drama (other
than the firestorm of sadness in my head).

Part of my therapy and rebuilding process involved getting in touch with more men. This was something that was
sorely lacking from my life for about the last ten years of my
first marriage. I spent the vast majority of my time being a
father and whatever was left was spent playing husband. My
therapist recognized this in me right away and suggested I
purposely reach out to men I knew to connect. Hang out.

Talk. So… I did!

I became close to a younger guy in my hometown, somebody that actually used to work with my ex-wife. We always hit it off when we saw each other at gatherings and functions, so he was one of the first people I contacted during my new mission to cultivate close guy friends. We hung out, drank beer, watched our favorite college sports team, played guitar… those were fantastic times. Of course, as any sane person would expect, I told him about what was going on at home. Like everyone else, he was in shock. He knew my ex and couldn't believe she was capable of such behavior.

Apparently, word got back to my ex-wife that I was hanging out with this former coworker of hers. She assumed, rightly so, that I was sharing personal stories of our pending divorce. This really set her off. Holy shit was she mad. She sent me a furious text letting me know that what happens between us is not the business of ex-coworkers of hers. She may have had a point, but this isn't something I can keep under wraps indefinitely. People will eventually want to know why we're not together and why the wife suddenly leaves her family!

I came home later that day to find the house looking like it had been robbed. A small table was knocked over. Pictures had been ripped from the walls, leaving spots of torn drywall behind. I imagine her leaving with a laundry basket full of her stuff as she clumsily runs into furniture, cursing my name on the way out of the house for the last time. The random sock and several pairs of her underwear leading to the front door paints a sad but hilarious picture in my mind. She left behind quite a bit. Mostly mementos from our past. Family photos. Kid stuff. Those items didn't have a role in the new chapter of her life.

I've heard this story from hundreds of guys over the years. Things go relatively smoothly… until the woman finds out that he said something to somebody's friend's cousin's former roommate who is a coworker of the wife. The husband is committing the cardinal sin of informing another human of exactly what is going on in their relationship. The wife, at best, has been on a campaign of telling everyone that you two *"just drifted apart,"* or, at worst, that you are a monster and completely to blame for the divorce. And then… the truth comes out. This pesky truth paints her in a less-than-stellar light, and she can't have that.

As I said in chapter two, what others think of your wife and her personal life is VERY important to her. It's not just cheating or divorcing wives who act this way. Pretty much every single woman who has ever existed is overly concerned about what her tribe may think of her. The current state of social media certainly doesn't help the situation. Every over-burdened mom spends hours per week posting photos and sharing stories that all point to the same conclusion: *"My kids are perfect, and I am a very hard-working wife and mom."* Mommy Martyrdom is the new online pandemic. She can bad-mouth herself to her group, but usually does so within the framework of victimhood.

Now you're turning a spotlight on the truth. Yeah… that's

not gonna end well.

HELL HATH NO FURY LIKE A WOMAN SCORNED

We have all heard this saying. I Googled the origin of the phrase. It dates back to a play written in the 1600s. It means, *"If you wrong a woman, you will see the worst of her. She will go on a rampage of anger to destroy you."* The most obvious example of this would be if a man cheats on his woman. She scratches *"CHEATER"* into the side of his car, sets his favorite guitar on fire, sells his motorcycle on Craig's List for ten dollars, posts pictures of him and his secret lover on Facebook, and texts all of his family members about what he's doing. Everyone sits back in shock and says the same thing: *"Wow... hell hath no fury..."*

So, why do you see such scorched-earth behavior from the woman that is leaving YOU? It's not the other way around. You don't want this. Hell, you've been hanging on for way too long trying to make it work. Again, you can't understand it. Don't try to understand it. Just try to get out of her way. Use the law where applicable. Is she saying things on Facebook to tarnish your reputation? That can hurt your professional reputation and cost you money in the long run. Get a lawyer to draw up a cease-and-desist order. Is she destroying your property? Call the police and get her arrested. Try your best to remove your emotions from the situation and see this as a legal and financial matter. She's a crazy little girl that is hurting and acting out the pain in the only way she knows how: By trying to hurt you. That's not your fault.

NOBODY CARES

When a man goes through a horrible divorce, especially one at the hands of a cheating and/or crazy wife, the man believes that everyone in his social group should stop what they are doing and fully appreciate what a deranged nut bagel his wife is… and how awesome, kind, and sweet he is.

Instead, he watches as his ex still goes to wine night with her friends, she still gets invited to the fall barbecue at Bob's house, her other friends donate her some free furniture for her new apartment, and other friends like her posts on Facebook where she shows off her new kitchen. *"What the hell is going on here?! Don't these people realize what she has done!? Why are they all acting like everything is normal?! Why is everyone on HER side?!"*

Newsflash my man. **Nobody cares.**

Yes, they care about you. Yes, they still like and love you as a friend. Yes, they wish nothing but the best for you, and yes, they probably know all about what your ex did and they really don't like it, and they feel bad for you having to go through this.

BUT, they don't want to be involved in your drama. They don't want to *"pick sides."* They have way more important things on their plates. They have jobs, kids, bills, and their own flavor of marital difficulties to contend with. Your situation was fodder for gossip talk around the kitchen table, but it never went beyond that. Yes, men that you know SHOULD probably tell their wives that hanging out with your ex is a bad idea (because of her negative influence on them), but be honest… how many of your guy friends have the cajones to actually put up those boundaries? Exactly.

Let it go, my man. Not everything revolves around you and your life. It's kinda like when somebody close to you dies. You have that sinking, awful gut feeling of loss. You go to the mall to buy a nice suit for the funeral, and everyone around you is normal and smiling. People are laughing. You almost want to yell out to everyone, *"I need you all to stop and join me in my sadness right now! You being all loud and happy is just very unsettling!"* They can all certainly empathize with your sadness, but that doesn't mean they have to mold their lives to fit your current suffering.

Everyone has their own shit to worry about. Yes, there is a bit of the *"damsel in distress"* thing going on. People may see your ex as being in distress and they are jumping up to help her. That's okay. That's human nature. Don't take it as a personal hit to you and your worth. They are free to do whatever they want. If their behavior dips too far into disrespectful territory and you see them blatantly approving of negative wife behavior, then delete them from your life. No big deal. People do stupid shit all the time. You can be equally indifferent to their drama.

YOU WILL DETACH

There was one aspect of my divorce that I wasn't really prepared for. It may sound like some kind of manly humble brag, but it's not. It's actually a statement on just how delicate our attachment to another human being can be. How fleeting the whole *"love"* thing is. What I'm talking about is how quickly I went from, *"I need to keep this woman and my family together,"* to, *"What in the hell was I thinking being with this woman all those years?"* Many of you will experience this same phenomenon. Your attachment to your ex will completely dissolve, and you'll feel like a magical spell has been lifted. In a way, that's exactly what happens.

When we first meet our women, they're usually presenting the most attractive version of themselves. They are flirty, feminine, sweet, and sexual. For many of us, we meet our wives when they are young and in the prime of their *"fertile female"* phase of life. One interesting aspect of men is we hold on to that image of our women throughout every phase of the relationship. Even when we are both in our eighties and withering away in a nursing home, we still see that sweet young thing we met all those many years ago.

Yes, women put a spell on us.

Another way of looking at it is the woman was a drug dealer that gave us the most potent and addictive drug imaginable. We go through the rest of the relationship chasing that high and hoping for just one more little taste. When we catch a glimpse of the old her, we fall right back into that old opium haze of love and lustfulness that caused us to commit to her years ago. It could be her walking across the room a certain way, wearing a certain outfit, laughing at your jokes, that cute little sneeze she has… or something blunt like the act of sex. All of these little and not so little things give you a taste of that old drug again.

Then, you separate. Your drug dealer is no longer available to you. No more drug for you. You go through withdrawals. You feel absolutely terrible. Your heart is pounding, your stomach is churning, you're not sleeping, the pounds are melting off your body… it's a horrendous experience. But then, the process is over. The fog of addiction lifts. You're clean.

Then you're left with a horrible feeling that all addicts in this position feel:

Regret.

"What in the Sam fuck was I thinking?!"

If you're like me, you weren't thinking. You were an addict just going through the motions. You were stuck in the machine of *"marriage and kids,"* combined with the lingering addiction of a guy who just wanted that little taste of being treated like a king again. As I've learned over the years, men will put up with A LOT just to get a glimpse of that early new relationship energy. I was no different.

After the separation, I was left with a lot of regret and a

lot of questions. Why did I overlook so many red flags at every stage of the relationship? Why did I put up with such a mundane relationship? Was I really attracted to my wife? Was she the type of person who made me pause and turn my head to get a better look? When I put down a list of must-haves for a future woman, does my ex have ANY of those qualities? No, no, and no? Then what in the hell was I thinking?

I wasn't. I was under a spell. I was chasing a high that, ironically, was impossible to get from my ex. Now that the spell has lifted, I can see that clearly. She was absolutely the wrong person to be with, and anyone with half a brain could see trouble on the horizon. Our divorce was inevitable.

CRAIG'S STORY

Craig's story was a little different from most. His divorce seemed to be truly amicable. The wife, Karen, struggled with depression for years after their kids were born. To her credit, she sought help in the form of therapy. Not only did she see a therapist on a weekly basis, but she also joined an informal support group of ladies all coping with postpartum depression. They would get together once a week for coffee or wine, talk about their issues, and be there for each other as they experienced the difficulties that often go along with life as a struggling mom.

Craig was very proud of his wife for all of her hard work. He knew of a couple of friends' wives who struggled with the same issues, and they didn't do any kind of work to overcome their depression. One friend ended up divorced, and the other is living in marital hell. That was also a big reason Karen ended up in therapy. She didn't want to be like THOSE women.

Part of Karen's therapy involved digging into her past life issues. Her *"family of origin"* struggles, as the professionals call it. Her own mother had issues with depression. Her father didn't cope well with the state of his marriage, and he took to drinking and infidelity to cope. This toxic cocktail of dysfunction led to Karen having a very anxiety-filled childhood. She brought that energy into adulthood and into her marriage with Craig.

After many hours of therapy and her talking to her support

group, Karen would realize that, while Craig was an amazing guy, he was no longer the right guy for her. If she was honest, she had fallen out of love with Craig after the birth of their first child. She was just hanging on by a thread. Craig knew it, too. He would routinely call her out on her change in behavior, and he pushed for both of them to get help. Craig chased Karen for the last eight years of their marriage.

With the fog of the depression and helplessness lifting, Karen was left with a relationship that she no longer felt excitement for. She no longer had the desire to connect with her partner. Whether it was colored by her depression or her childhood baggage, the fact was that Craig was now a symbol of a lot of resentment and negativity in Karen's life. She recognized that it was not all his fault. He was dropped into the life of Karen 1.0, and now Karen 2.0 no longer needed or wanted him.

The couple attended a few marriage counseling sessions, but they just delayed the inevitable. They had one last heart-to-heart chat. They both agreed that yes, the marriage had come to an end. It had actually ended years ago. They were both just too scared to pull the trigger on the separation. There was no need to point fingers and lay blame. It was what it was. They were going to divorce.

The divorce was friendly, business-like, and void of any drama. Their kids handled the news well. Mom and dad still got together occasionally for some outings and even had dinner together once per week as a family. While some may say that this was unhealthy and would lead to some form of lingering attachment, they both saw it as a healthy exercise in showing the kids just how two people can get along, even after they break up.

But, all was not so simple. Three weeks after their divorce was finalized, Karen started seeing somebody. It was a guy from her work. Craig was first made aware of the new boyfriend because he saw a pair of men's sneakers next to the front door in Karen's apartment. Craig said nothing, but he knew what it meant. Karen had moved on. Not only had she moved on, but it was serious enough for a man to leave a pair of shoes behind. That signified comfort. Familiarity. Had this relationship been going on prior to the divorce?

Craig emailed me and booked an appointment to chat. He was doing so well. Everything was cordial and smooth during the divorce and the immediate aftermath. Craig himself wasn't ready to date anyone just yet and told himself that he would give it six months before even considering it. While he was actually feeling great, there was still a part of him that recognized he wasn't ready yet. Seeing those sneakers made him well aware that this whole divorce thing was far more traumatic than he thought.

Craig's voice was shaky when we spoke over Zoom. He was embarrassed and trying to hold back tears, like many guys do. I tried to reassure him, *"You know, it's perfectly okay to feel emotion during all of this. Jesus, you're a human being, dude. You've been through a lot. Your marriage ended. That's a huge freakin' deal."* He wiped away a tear and said that he knew, but he was just so shocked at how much a single pair of Nikes affected him. *"I knew it was going to happen one day, but I didn't think it would be this soon. Kind of a kick in the gut."*

It would take a while, but Craig could eventually see those shoes and other garments lying around Karen's apartment without it triggering anxiety. He eventually met the new boyfriend and even admitted that he was an *"okay dude."*

CHAPTER 4
THE RELATIONSHIP GAME

DATING AGAIN

Thinking about dating again? Ready to get back in the saddle? You're probably not ready. I've talked to so many guys who made the mistake of jumping into the dating world way too soon after their separations/divorces from their wives. They will tell me how it's *"been a long time"* since they have had sex (dead bedroom marriages are common before divorce) and they just want to get their natural male sexual urges out of their systems. Maybe they just want that close, intimate connection with a woman again. Maybe they long for a real-life companion. What they later discover is that they are trying to use women as a psychological band-aid to cover up the massive gaping wound left by their exes. They feel incomplete. They are conditioned to have a woman by their side when going through life. They miss sharing life and their day-to-day routines. They miss the little inside jokes. They miss the partnership. These are the men that fall in love VERY quickly with the first girl that makes goo-goo eyes at them, more often than not with disastrous results.

If you're reading this book, you are most likely not ready to date. You are still in too much pain and too broken to bring another human being into your life. It's not fair to you, to your family, or to the person you are dating. The manic high you will experience when the first woman shows interest in you will be drowned out by the intense low you will feel when it all comes crashing down and ends horribly. You will take one step forward and nineteen steps back. You'll end up worse off than you are now.

You ain't ready, amigo. Trust me.

But if you're like the vast majority of the men I help, you won't listen to my advice. You'll put up an online dating account or go hang out at the singles bar. Probably both. You'll either become disgusted and depressed about the shallowness of the dating landscape (and the lack of attention you will receive), or you'll become elated at how easily you can get attention and affection from decent looking, seemingly normal women. Regardless of the outcome, if you're like 100% of the men I help, you'll later wish you had waited a while longer before jumping into the dating pool. These men come back to me with their tails between their legs, saying, *"Well, that was stupid."* Hey, people have to learn the hard way. It's human nature. I understand completely. I was one of them.

If you plan on entering the dating world, you need to be aware of just how NOT *"normal"* and wholesome of an experience it is. You need to know that it is, in fact, a giant stupid game. You need to know the rules, the customs, and the culture of the stupid game before you jump into it headfirst. If you go in blind, you'll just end up as another piece of roadkill on the dating highway.

Do yourself a favor and throw away all your past conceptions of what dating is. Whatever you do, don't bring into this world your notions of *"comfort"* and *"being in a relationship"* that you cultivated while you were married. That world in your mind has nothing to do with this new world you're about to dive into. This is dating. If you had prior experience with dating (years ago before you were married), you can throw out all that experience as well. Dating is nowhere near the same as it used to be. Not even close. To be honest, you were probably wrong about the dating game back then, too. That might be part of what got you into this mess.

THE UGLY TRUTH OF THE MODERN-DAY MATING GAME

The human mating game begins with, and is primarily based upon, basic animalistic attraction. It's visual. We want what looks good to us. The entire process starts with *"Whoa. Who is THAT over there?"* In today's online dating landscape, this "shallow" visual mindset is more obvious than ever. Don't think for one second that the "good" women in online dating see right past your looks and dig deeper into your profile to discover your "true" good qualities. Sorry, no. It's never been that way and never will be that way. Your looks get you in the door.

There's a somewhat disturbing oh-so-true phenomenon that society has known for generations now, but we haven't really quantified to any specific degree. We all know this to be true, but we never could put a real number on it. Now, thanks to the anonymous data-driven nature of the internet, we have the numbers to illustrate the ugly truth:

• Women find 80% of the men on the dating market to be completely unattractive.

• Men have a much more *"fair"* distribution of who are attractive, average, and unattractive.

The conclusion is that women are very picky. Men… not so much. Again, we all knew this already. Men will bang almost anything that gives them the time of day, and women will try to hold out for the best possible man they can get. Men have to put on a show of qualifying themselves to earn the reward of a woman's time. The women in question don't have to be super-attractive top-tier women, either. We all know super-high-value men that routinely sleep with objectively sub-par women. The super stud had needs. The below-average gal from the bar was available, so they had sex.

To summarize, women from the complete spectrum of the attraction scale get access to the top-tier men (sexually). Whether she's a perfect ten or the homely housekeeper, she has a chance. They have a buffet of mate choices. Men will take what they can get. The menu is limited for them. Yes, the mating game is, and always has been, a woman's market.

Even with the data in our faces, people will disagree: *"Yes, but if that were true, then why are all these women marrying men left and right? If they only liked 20% of the guys at a visceral attraction level, then there aren't enough guys to go around and very few women would be in relationships and eventually marry."*

The answer is simple: Women often settle. To fulfil their desire to have babies and attain financial and emotional security, women will "settle" for a man that is in the 80% group. She can weigh the pros and cons and convince herself that he is *"good enough."* Sure, she longs for the 20% guy with the great looks, personality, and charisma that makes her underwear fly off… but that's obviously super rare in a guy and it's not realistic. If she wants to start up that family life she always dreamed about, she better set aside her dreams of the knight in shining armor and give those good-but-not-perfect guys a chance. Unfortunately, this common theme of *"settling"* or *"giving up"* on finding Mr. Perfect keeps some women operating with a consistent undercurrent of resentment. *"Nothing I do is ever good enough for her,"* men in these relationships will often say. It's true. The man had two strikes against him before he even stepped up to the plate. He feels like he has to consistently qualify himself and prove his worth, because he does.

DON'T MAKE DATING AND MARRIAGE YOUR LIFE'S MISSION

Dating should only be approached as a fun diversion in life. It should be ancillary to your mission, your friends, your self-care, and your family. Dating should never be approached with the endgame in mind of marriage and attaining Real Love. You just want to meet nice, fun, and attractive women to spend time with. That's it. You want to go into this with the mindset of a Mentally Healthy Non-Needy Man (MHNNM).

The MHNNM realizes that most women he dates will not be long-term relationship material. They won't even come close. There will be varying degrees of broken women, mentally ill women, and really good women who, unfortunately, were never given the tools to learn how to be successful in a long-term relationship. A chosen few MAY be up for the job as his life partner, but they will be the rare exception to the rule.

The MHNNM may eventually decide to try out a monogamous relationship with a seemingly good woman. If he does so, he keeps his eyes and ears open for signs that her behavior would be detrimental to his wellbeing. If real red flags are detected, he hits the eject button and bails out of the relationship with no hesitation and no animosity. *"I like you a lot. I appreciate your time. But this isn't going to work out for me. I wish you nothing but the best."*

Unfortunately, what many experienced MHNNM men will tell you is that they hit that eject button over and over… and it grows tiresome. Eventually, they grow cynical and lose faith in the whole monogamous process. They tell their dates right up front, *"Just so you know, I'm not interested in a serious long-term relationship."* It's honest, mature, and refreshing, but also a huge disappointment to many women looking to settle down with a great guy they caught in an ocean of awful men. *"All men care about is sex with no commitment,"* *they will say.*

It's not that the men don't want to commit, or that they have an unnatural *"fear of commitment"* (a common shaming tactic by women in the MHNNM's social circle). The vast majority of men that I talk to have a genuine desire to be in a comfortable, long-term relationship with the woman of their dreams. Unfortunately, that woman remains in their dreams, and she's rarely found out in the real world. It's not a matter of being *"unrealistic"* or having *"ridiculously high standards,"* as many people will tell the bachelor (a projection of the common female mindset), but it's instead a matter of recognizing that mental illness, poor life choices, terrible childhoods, laziness, several illegitimate children, and lack of ambition are all signs of a person who is not suitable for the extremely important and difficult job of *"life partner."* They could be a great friend, they may be great for the occasional date or fun, but they're not somebody you say, *"I do,"* to. That's just asking for a shit ton of trouble, as many of us later learn years down the line.

It's the poor quality of the female partner candidates that keeps the MHNNM in perpetual bachelorhood. The MHNNM recognizes the life-ruining power that the wrong woman can have, so he treads very carefully. He's not desperate. He's not one of the 80% that is DYING for female attention and will gladly hand over his time and resources to them. The MHNNM never settles. He never brushes red flags under the rug and hopes they go away. This is a perfectly healthy mindset, and not one worthy of any shame or guilt.

DON'T BE ASHAMED TO BE THE MHNNM

A lot of men are conditioned to feel guilty about just *"having fun"* and dating without hastily committing long-term to one woman. After all, what do we mean when we say we are just interested in *"having fun"*? We mean having sex and going out on dates. It means doing all the fun stuff without throwing the proverbial monkey wrench into the machine and watching it explode, just so that you can check off *"in a committed relationship"* from your to-do list. It means maintaining sanity, having fun, and doing what we can to fulfill our emotional and physical needs, while still maintaining our life mission and our dignity.

Contrary to popular belief, most men do not want to feel like some kind of sexual-predator-douchebag that is simply interested in sex with a buffet of strange women. The MHNNM doesn't want to be seen as the guy who has zero regard for women's emotions. They just want to be honest, drama-free and, yes, have their needs met... but they still strive to be decent human beings with good hearts. Society will tell the MHNNM again and again that it's an impossible task.

Trying to maintain this good-hearted single MHNNM persona is really difficult for most guys. It certainly doesn't help that all the women (and even some men) in a man's life are browbeating him and attempting to shame him into a more *"stable"* and comfortable life with one woman. *"When are you going to settle down and meet a nice girl?"* mom will say at Christmas dinner. *"You know, a real man wouldn't date a bunch of girls... he would commit to one. Like that Mary gal you were dating last year. She was a doll!"* Aunt Teresa will say while you're waiting in line for birthday cake. Every MHNNM hears it again and again. Why are all of the people in his life doing this? What are they REALLY trying to tell him? Why is it that being a single man and having fun is such a turnoff to so many people in his social circle?

What they are all really telling you is that they would much prefer you be seen in the comfortable *"safer,"* more *"respect-ful,"* and more *"productive"* role as the Provider. They don't want to see you as a sexual being. They don't want to think of their son/nephew/cousin/brother as the *"Lover"* who jumps from woman to woman and doesn't truly contribute to society overall (based on their own preconceptions of personal value and what *"contribution"* entails).

LOVER VS. PROVIDER

In the mating game, we can categorize men in one of two ways: He is the Lover, or he is the Provider. It's not a tough concept to wrap your mind around. We all know Lovers and Providers in our own lives. Maybe we called them Jocks and Dorks in high school. Popular Guys and Nerds. Alpha Males and Beta Males. Bad Boys and Nice Guys. Whatever you call it, we all innately know what it means. It's a phenomenon as old as time.

The Lover is the fun guy. He's the guy that a girl may date and have lots of crazy sex with, but she probably wouldn't ever bring him home to meet mom and dad. She may show him off to friends, follow him on social media, have long sexting sessions with him, be sexually open and experimental with him, and skip work or class just to see him… but the idea of marriage and long-term commitment may not even be on the radar with the Lover. Often, the Lover is actually a bit of a loser. He could live on a mattress on the floor of his parents' basement, drive a shitty car, and be *"in between jobs"*… but there is something about the guy that drives the women crazy. It could be his looks. His charisma. His charm. His abundance of confidence. Whatever the indescribable *"IT"* is, he's got it in spades. He's a natural.

The Provider is the safe bet. He's the stable guy. He's the one that will probably make a great dad and always be there for his future wife. If you're a woman, you definitely want to bring this guy home to mom and dad. *"See? I know how to pick a good guy! Isn't he the ideal husband you always had in mind for me?!"* The Provider looks absolutely perfect on paper. He checks all the boxes. He's good looking enough. He's super nice. He wants to start a family. He has a career. So, what's the problem? The problem is that the Provider is just not a sexy man. At all. He doesn't have that indescribable "it" factor. There's no oomph there. There's no *"I would drive four hours in a blizzard just to spend the night with him"* there. Nature is not screaming, *"BREED WITH THIS HUNK OF A MAN. MAKE BABY. NOW. BEFORE HE GETS AWAY."* Instead, nature is whispering to the woman, *"He'll probably do a great job of taking care of you and your children."*

In evolutionary terms, it's not unheard of for the Lover to make the babies and for the Provider to take care of them. Modern scientific advances in cheap DNA testing like 23andMe.com have brought this sad fact to light. Endless Tinder profiles with pregnant twenty-something girls looking for a *"real man"* to settle down with and *"no more games"* show the Lover/Provider dynamic in action. The Lover had his fun. Now she needs a Provider to clean up the mess.

The Provider is the guy who frequently complains about his awful married sex life. He's the guy who says that his wife switched off the sex supply and got fat as soon as she said, *"I do,"* pulling the marital *"bait and switch"* routine on him. The Provider longs for passion and lustfulness from his wife. The lack of intimacy and validation kills him inside. He truly loves his wife with all of his heart. He probably has an unhealthy worship of her. He can't fathom cheating on his wife or divorcing her, so he attempts to remedy the situation by trying to appeal to his wife's rational side. He will often have sit-down conversations with her and point out that his physical needs aren't being met. *"I love you, but it's like you don't even LIKE me anymore,"* he may say. The *"Big Talk"* usually just makes things exponentially worse. He is bringing to light the uncomfortable truth that every woman in his wife's position doesn't want to verbalize, much less hear from her own Provider husband: She is just not turned on by him. She settled for him. That's just how it is.

The Provider's frigid wife also has very real human sexual needs. They are also not being met. She's miserable. Yet she will rarely admit this out of fear of losing her Provider. Her sexual atomic bomb will remain undercover and dormant until the day her psychological boundaries are down, and the sexual engine is fired up again. This is normally done with a new Lover.

"I'M NOT LIKE THAT ANYMORE"

Here is a common scenario (thanks to the internet) that further illustrates the difference between Lovers and Providers:

A man in a stable but boring marriage discovers the surprisingly kinky and promiscuous past of what he thought all along was a sexually dull and inexperienced wife. Maybe he found an old USB thumb drive tucked away in a closet and on it was a video of his wife having a threesome with a man and another woman. Maybe he found a series of sexually graphic photos of his wife from several years ago posted on the internet for all to see. Maybe he found a diary or blog

with all the sordid details of boyfriends past and their amazing sexual escapades. In these sexual mementos from years
gone by, she is being free and fun, doing sexual things she
says she said she would never ever do with her husband because they are *"gross," "silly,"* or *"only for the fake porn people
because nobody in real life does stuff like that."*

The result is the Provider quickly realizes what his role is
and always has been in his wife's life, and he feels completely
fooled and humiliated. He is both boiling with anger and incredibly sad at the same time. He always hoped that HE was
the guy that would have the power to bring out his wife's
animalistic sexual side, not some LOSER from her past.
He feels like he has been playing the part of the chump this
whole time. He gets the privilege of devoting all of his time,
energy, love, and resources to the spouse and gets relatively
little genuine physical intimacy and sexual validation in
return. Douchebag McLoserface from college got to have
multiple threesomes with her and she SURE seemed to like
oral sex back then (along with everything else on the sexual
menu).

Once he gets up the nerve to approach his wife with the
newfound evidence of her past, she will do her best to put
him at ease. She was just in a *"young phase of her life back
then,"* she will explain. She may say that she felt *"pressured"*
to do those things in college because she was young, immature, and thought she would lose her asshole loser of a
boyfriend if she didn't do the threesome, give him oral sex,
or pose for all those photos that were posted on the internet.
The husband listens, but he can't drop it. He keeps drilling

away with more questions. *"Ok, then what about the pizza guy that Deb told me all about? Did you feel pressure to fuck him, too?! How about the guy you banged while on the trip to France your freshman year? Or the guy in Spain who wore the matador cape while he banged you at the pool party??"* As his questions and accusations keep coming, his wife's anger builds. What does it matter what she did back then? This is NOW, and she loves HIM, not all those losers from her past. She has matured since then. That was YEARS ago. She's a completely different person now. She's a mom and his devoted wife. She chose HIM. He should appreciate and respect that. She shouldn't be judged by some experimental phase in her life.

With every explanation she gives, the wife just digs herself deeper and deeper into a hole that she won't be able to climb out of. She did the most personal and physically vulnerable acts with people that were losers compared to her husband. She didn't form close, intimate bonds with them like she did with him. She didn't have children with them. Those men weren't there for her when she had her breast cancer scare, or when she gained sixty pounds with her pregnancy. This makes her husband, in his mind, less than a loser. He doesn't possess the qualities needed to elicit the same sexual response from the wife he loves more than anyone on Earth. He's completely crushed, and the wife just doesn't seem to get it.

Her lack of empathy towards her husband is completely baffling to him. He's probably never felt a deeper sense of betrayal than in this moment, and his wife's only solution is to further blame him for even questioning her sexual past and current relationship motives. Yet, everything she says just points to the same conclusion: The other guy(s), along with the free and fun atmosphere of her youth, elicited a level of consistent and heightened sexual energy that marriage and dear boring husband cannot spark for even a few seconds. She was a free, wild, happy, and animalistic girlfriend with THEM… and an asexual boring mom with HIM. He's had to endure years of, *"I just feel fat and gross and don't want to do anything,"* and, *"Can you just give it a rest for one night?"* Those guys from her past just had to show up with some beer and a pizza and she was the instant star in a real-life porn movie.

He is the Provider… those other men were her Lovers. Age and maturity have nothing to do with it, as many guys like him learn after discovering their wives in a torrid love affair with a douchebag just like the ones they *"outgrew"* from their fun and free pasts.

THE ELUSIVE LOVER+PROVIDER MAN

The ideal guy for a woman is one that has both Lover and Provider qualities. He's the charming, ambitious, and good-looking guy with the heart of gold. He's the fun, friendly, but slightly dangerous guy that other women fantasize about. Women don't look at him and say, *"I wish I could fool him into marrying and providing for me."* Instead, they say, *"I wish he would PICK ME!"* See the difference? The ideal man is a prize that has his pick of the litter. Think of the TV show The Bachelor. Women don't settle for the Bachelor (the successful and handsome young guy with perfect hair). They win him. In fact, oddly enough, they don't mind sharing him, as we learn when watching the Bachelor make out and eventually sleep with girl after girl, only to have them all cry when he doesn't hand them the coveted rose that keeps them on the show. If they get to have time alone with Prince Charming, and possibly win him in the end, then they can turn a blind eye to all the other *"dates"* he has with the other pretty contestants.

Like the elusive, beautiful unicorn of a woman who has a good heart, solid boundaries, and coping skills that serve her well in a long-term relationship, the good all-around Lover+Provider guy is VERY rare and in VERY high demand. A high-value unicorn of a woman usually snags a prime relationship candidate like that early on. Unfortunately for most thirty-plus-year-old post-divorce women in the dating game (most single women you will encounter), they quickly realize that finding the good all-around L+P guy is damn near impossible. That leaves women with two options: Lover OR Provider. They just can't seem to find both wrapped together in one man.

Single women will probably dabble on both sides of the Lover/Provider fence during their dating careers. If they're still in their fertile twenties, they may likely date solely on the Lover side. Life for young women is primarily about FUN and self-discovery, after all. Like most young people, they fall into the stupid *"forever young"* mentality and put partying and making money ahead of the boring stuff like finding a life partner and making babies. Because of this mindset, they will listen solely to their young libido, and that libido is telling them to go for the Lovers that make them swoon, not the Providers you bring home to mom.

But, as we all know, life has a way of sneaking up on you pretty damn fast. The next thing you know, you're a woman celebrating your thirtieth birthday. Everything changes. Your body is not the same. Who is this person in the mirror? Why does my back hurt? Why are my arms suddenly flabby? To make matters worse, it seems like all your friends are married and having babies. Your parents are constantly pressuring you to settle down, which is the last thing you need to hear. *"Yeah, like it's so easy for a thirty-year-old woman to find a perfect life partner! You just go to the husband store and pick one out, right?!"* Then, in what feels like just a few short years later, you're suddenly forty. You're left wondering what in the hell just happened. This isn't funny anymore. This is downright depressing.

This is the sad reality for many single women in the modern dating game.

THE CAREER GAL

More than a few women in my social circle find themselves with great careers but no prospects for a long-term *"Real Love"* relationship, let alone concrete plans for having children they so desperately NEED to have. With the biological clock screaming at them, these women finally wake up and start dating with the goal of finding a long-term partner. They make the mistake of overestimating the quality of the male dating pool (L+P men are very rare) AND they over-estimate their own value as a partner. When somebody asks them what their own positive qualities are, they list their PhDs, their awesome careers, their apartments in the city, and the vacation condos in Florida. They're ironically taking a page from the Provider book of dating tips, and they think it will get them the perfect Lover+Provider partner they so assuredly *"deserve."*

Nope. Not gonna happen.

Most of the Lover+Provider guys are off the market. They may have already settled into stable relationships back in their twenties, or they have been around the block more than a few times and know the rules of the game. In the mind of the L+P man, there's zero incentive to partner with the typical single thirty-plus-year-old gal who finally needs to *"settle down"* and make a family. In the shallow and unfair world of the dating game, the aging but single L+P guy can actually gain access to the top tier of the female attrac-tiveness pyramid. He can still snag the twenty-something attractive women who are just starting out on their rela-tionship journeys. He has his pick of the litter… and Sally, the thirty-eight-year-old Vice President of Sales for Acme Corporation making $200K per year, is not even in the run-ning. Instead, he dates the cute and bubbly barista who just recently graduated college and still lives with her parents. It's not because the older woman's career is intimidating. Her career is a complete non-factor.

It's not *"fair."* It sucks for the good and honest women who have worked hard and have a lot to offer in a relationship with a good man. But, this is dating. This is the mating game. It's never been fair. It can be unbelievably cruel… as you will probably soon find out for yourself.

NO LOVER+PROVIDER GUYS AVAILABLE? TIME FOR PLAN B

"Where have all the good men gone?!" women will scream. Translation, *"Where are the good Lover+Provider guys that I feel like I genuinely deserve?"* If they can't find the very rare Lover+Provider guy, they will move on to the next best thing: The Super Provider. This change in direction widens their dating pool significantly. Instead of putting things like attractiveness, personality, and sexual compatibility at the front of the *"must have"* list, you will see items like job, money, social status, health, and agreeableness at the forefront. Simply put, she's looking for a financially dominant but emotionally submissive man. This man, much like an actor in a movie, is filling a role in her life plan. She's the director of this movie, and she needs an actor with specific qualifications and skills… and they must also be good at taking direction. She has had this life plan in place for many years, and just because she's now past her prime and short on husband candidates doesn't mean it won't happen. Oh, it will happen, even if that means doing things like setting aside her sexual needs or giving up completely on the dream of landing the one Lover+Provider guy. If push comes to shove, she can get her Lover needs met elsewhere.

Unlike what a lot of men may like to believe, most of these

"desperate" women don't end up with twelve cats and a drinking problem. Most end up married. Make no mistake, there is a bevy of male Super Providers more than ready and willing to scoop up a desperate single woman and play the part of her hero.

A LOT OF MEN ARE ONLY COMFORTABLE IN THE PROVIDER ROLE

A typical recently divorced man will create an online dating profile (or two, or three) and immediately highlight his Provider qualities. This is the natural game plan that they have fallen back on for years. If he's ever been asked what makes him a good husband, he instantly points out his Provider traits. He's great with kids. He coaches all of their teams. He has a stable job with a good income. He can keep a house clean and well-maintained. He's the kind of guy who loves helping people out when they need it. He's your quintessential "nice guy," in other words.

What is he NOT saying with all of this nice guy Provider behavior? *"I'm a sexual guy who likes to have fun and I know my worth."* This is precisely what the Lover does. The Lover, in action and words, conveys the theme of, *"I'm awesome. Take it or leave it. I really don't give a shit what you think."* The Provider is just like those South American birds you see on the nature shows, doing his little dance while fluffing his feathers and showing off the nest he made while the female stands on her perch feigning interest. *"Pick me! Pick me! Please!"* This is exactly what most men do when dating today. They're telling the women of the world that they

KNOW they're not worth much on their own without all their resources. They have nothing other than their Provider qualities to showcase to would-be girlfriends. They might as well provide their credit card numbers, bank statements and sperm counts instead of headshots on their dating profiles.

So, what if you really DO want to play the part of Provider and you don't feel at all comfortable in the Lover role? Well, then I strongly suggest you find a good hobby, get a dog, and leave dating alone until you grow into a more well-rounded man. Why? Because you WILL be chewed up and tossed aside like the resource machine that you are. You WILL have your heart crushed and your wallet drained. You WILL be worse off than you were before. It may take years, but it will happen. That's just the way it is in the modern-day relationship game. Nice guys do, in fact, finish last.

WHAT'S IN STORE FOR THE PROVIDER IN A RELATIONSHIP

Once the single woman achieves her goal of landing the Provider, it won't take much time before resentment grows and her feelings of being spiritually, emotionally, and sexually unfulfilled grow as well. This is when wives close the sexual gates (*"Not tonight, I have a headache"*), seem to be perpetually angry (nothing you do is ever good enough for her), spend way too much money, and gain fifty pounds. They're not happy. They're miserable. They're trying to fill a void. They're coping. Nothing about this marriage turned out how they thought it would. The movie is not going according to plan, and the director is pissed off. That's when it's time to fire some actors. As you probably know, it only takes one person in the relationship to step away and call it quits. It's not put up to a democratic vote.

Remember, women file 70 – 80% of all divorces. They have no hesitation in hitting the eject button. The Provider is always the one left wondering what in the hell just happened. He did everything right! He played by the imaginary book of rules that he was taught his whole life, and in the end, it bit him on the ass.

If it helps push the point, think of what your marriage would be like if you settled for a really nice, kind-hearted woman that was four hundred pounds and looked like John Madden. She may be a brilliant conversationalist, may be an awesome friend, and she may be the best mom on the planet… but you would always have this awful ugly cloud hanging over your head. You married an objectively hideous beast of a human being. She doesn't turn you on in the slightest. In fact, she repulses you. You yourself aren't bad looking, and other WAY more attractive women flirt with you, and they even sometimes bluntly ask you, *"What on EARTH are you doing with HER?!"*

Sound like a marriage made in heaven? Sound like something that has long-term potential? Of course not. Eventually, the man will go crazy or start having emotional and physical affairs with other women… all because something crucial (physical attraction) is missing from his relationship. This is precisely how the woman married to a Provider feels. There's something crucial missing, and she will eventually grow resentful of the mismatch and find ways to fill the void.

THE SEARCH FOR REAL LOVE

Until now, a romantic relationship and finding the coveted gold ring of *"Real Love"* is probably something that you haven't put a lot of time, thought, or planning into. You probably believe that it eventually *"just happens"* to most men, much like catching a cold or taking a dump. *"Men date a little, find the love of their lives, get married and have kids. That's just the way it is,"* readers will often tell me. They tell me romantic stories about how their grandparents met and are still together so many decades later. Grandpa saw Grandma at the corner store buying candy when they were both twelve years old. He knew right then and there he would marry her, and he eventually did. It's been sunshine, rainbows and lots of grandkids ever since.

Many men don't treat finding new relationship partners like the dramatic life-changing experiences that they truly are. In fact, men will put more time into finding the right car with the right options than they will finding a partner for life. When car hunting, they'll research different models, compare used versus new, look at different financing options, look at the additional cost of the heated seats and rear-facing camera, consider an extended warranty, etc. With a relationship, they simply fall for that cute girl that showed them interest one time.

"Hey, Sally from accounting is cute, and she likes me. Cool. Wonder what she'd be like as a wife...."

Unlike what popular culture tells us, men are hopeless romantics in relationships. Any hint of pragmatism goes out the window when it comes to interacting with the fairer sex. Most men truly feel that Real Love just miraculously falls from the sky. They also feel that women think in the same way.

They couldn't be more wrong.

WHAT IS "REAL LOVE"?

Real Love is a choice. Real Love is sacrifice. Real Love is something that two people have to work hard to achieve and maintain throughout the course of a long-term relationship. Real Love lasts a lifetime. Real Love is extremely rare. You may not experience true Real Love in your lifetime.

Oh sure, you will experience a crush, overwhelming lust, and nervous butterflies over a girl. We all have that from time to time. The feelings may be reciprocated, and you may end up in a monogamous relationship that will last years. You may have kids, a mortgage, shared assets, etc. The delicate nature of your relationship eventually shows its ugly self when shit hits the fan or something transforms the dynamic of your relationship. It could be something simple, like a job change or the death of a parent. Sometimes that is all it takes to get the divorce train rolling. The boundaries are broken down and a series of psychological events change your spouse's mindset completely. One minute you're thinking about what to make the kids for dinner, and the next minute your wife is crying about how she just doesn't have feelings for you anymore.

It happens.

Sorry if this happened to you, but what you had wasn't Real Love. It was a chapter in your life that resulted in a lot of great memories and a lot of sadness. You're not the first to think he was in a Real Love relationship, and you won't be the last. We've all been fooled. Such is life.

THE TIMELINE OF A GOOD REAL LOVE RELATIONSHIP

• Super strong mutual physical attraction.

• Flirting. Getting to know each other. Sex. Strong sexual compatibility.

• *"Wow, I really like this person a great deal. Both inside and out. I'd like to try a monogamous relationship with them."*

• Years of a strong relationship.

• Genuine love, respect, and appreciation. Growing closer together. True partnership.

• Marriage.

• Children.

• Struggle. Bad Times.

• Enduring love and devotion.

• Grand kids. Great grand kids.

• Death.

It's somewhere around the *"struggle"* part where a lot of relationships are exposed for what they really are. The men I talk to are proud to say that they stuck it out and worked hard during the really tough times of their marriages. Unfortunately, with hindsight being 20/20, the man realizes that the tough times are exactly when things went south for his wife. She just wasn't nearly as tough as he thought she was. He later learns that nobody ever taught her how to cope when shit hit the fan. She also never learned the concept of *"boundaries"* while growing up. She was far too pliable with her emotions, bending whichever way the wind blew. Eventually, she was mentally overwhelmed by the inevitable awfulness and boredom that life dishes out to all of us. She attempted to relieve her anxieties in the worst way. She let nature and her compulsions take over.

She may have shopped until the credit cards maxed out. She may have eaten until she gained one hundred pounds. She may have texted her ex-boyfriend and sent him nude photos. She may have had an affair with her asshole coworker. These things are forms of self-medicating and attempts to drown out what she innately knows: She doesn't have it in her to maintain a Real Love relationship. She's just not cut out for it. She doesn't have the right tools in her mental toolbox. She's just a common broken human being.

Contrary to popular belief, Real Love is not for all of us. It's funny how we are quick to say, *"Running a marathon is not for me"* or, *"Being a rocket scientist is not for me,"*… but I'll be damned if nearly everyone doesn't think they have a RIGHT to a long-term Real Love relationship. A combination of peer/family pressure and Hollywood fiction have convinced us that falling for somebody and being together forever and ever is the magic endgame for absolutely everyone. Yes, everyone knows about the awful divorce statistics, but what's the first thing we all say when somebody breaks up? *"You'll find somebody again! Trust me!"* We treat the end goal of finding a Real Love life partner just like going to the bathroom or eating food. It's a given that you need it and will find it.

For most people, Real Love is just too damn hard to maintain. It takes two to tango, as they say. What most don't tell you is that it takes an entire family and social circle to help you keep the relationship machine humming away as well. Unfortunately, you can't just assume that all of your partner's family and friends will have your relationship's best interests in mind. If your spouse is dangling on the edge of the divorce cliff, more than a few people close to her are waiting to gleefully push her right on over and watch her plummet to her inevitable relationship death. In today's society, there is a chorus of people that will cheer on your wife's poor decisions. They will give the worst advice that ends up dramatically ending your marriage, much to the confusion of the betrayed husband. What you don't see is that your wife is a beacon of hope for her bored friends who dream of saying, *"Fuck it,"* and walking away from their own god-awful marriages. They will live vicariously through your wife's bad girl behavior and enjoy every drama-filled moment.

As I mentioned in chapter two, there are just far too many temptations out there today. They make holding on to Real Love that much harder. The good news is that all of these temptations are an excellent way to weed out the bad relationship candidates. The relationships that are left are as strong as you can get. They can endure just about anything, and they recognize the power they have when working together as a team. That's everyone's dream.

The bad news is that this relationship dynamic represents a tiny portion of the population. Your wayward wife, statistically, was not meant to be in a Real Love relationship. Most of us don't find out until after several kids and many years go by. As you now know, most poor relationship candidates don't show their true selves until shit hits the fan.

Remember: **Most relationship candidates are, in fact, BAD Real Love relationship candidates.**

EVERY MAN THINKS HE CAN WIN THE RELATIONSHIP LOTTERY

Finding and nurturing a Real Love relationship means that a lot of different things need to happen:

1. Finding somebody you are insanely physically attracted to, and vice versa.

2. Discovering that you are sexually compatible.

3. Learning that you are emotionally, intellectually, and spiritually compatible.

4. Both of you are tough, have good coping skills, and will work through obstacles that life throws at you together as a team.

5. Both of you have a good sense of boundaries and can resist temptation and compulsive behavior for the good of the partnership and the family.

Note the use of the term *"BOTH."* Real Love is not a one-person job. Both people have to work in tandem. Both people have to put in the time and effort. It takes two people to marry, but it only takes one person to divorce. The one strong person is not enough to keep things afloat. Yes, I'm talking to you, Mr. Fixer-Upper guy. You can't fix a broken relationship all by yourself.

If you DO find Real Love and you go to your death bed knowing you found your soul mate… congratulations. You won the love lottery. There is absolutely, positively nothing better in life. I wish everyone in the world could experience Real Love. It's a magical thing. For the vast majority of you reading this, you will not find it. I know that's really tough to hear, but it's the truth. I'm not going to bullshit you. You get enough of that from everyone else in your life.

Staying with the lottery analogy, you're going to keep buying scratch-off tickets hoping to quit your job and buy that fancy house with the Ferrari in the garage. Sure, now and then you may scratch off a $500 winner. It's just enough to keep you coming back for more. In the end, the casino always wins. You would've been better off investing that money in yourself. Instead of spending money and time on rolling the relationship dice, you should've joined a gym, invested your cash, and helped your community. In the long run, this usually ends up being a cheaper and far more rewarding course of action. Ironically, this is also the course of action that is more likely to lead to a Real Love relationship.

YOU DON'T NEED REAL LOVE

You need to remove from your head the mentality of: *"I need to find Real Love or else I'm a failure in life."* It is just setting yourself up for a miserable life of chasing the promise of the elusive paradise. When men have the end goal of *"Real Love"* in mind, they put up blinders to all the nagging little and not-so-little bad things about our mate we like to call "red flags." All those warning signs that say, *"Uh oh, this will not end well for you, dude. Take action now,"* are ignored for the greater good of maintaining course to reach the coveted destination of Real Love. It's like the Titanic trying to make record time across the Atlantic and ignoring all the warnings about icebergs in the water. How'd that turn out for them?

The whole mindset of: *"Must find partner, get house, have kid before I am thirty five,"* is the typical (and understandable) mindset of a single woman. By no means should you feel pressured to follow suit. Women have the all-powerful biological clock ticking (their growing need for kids along with lowering fertility as they get older) and the consistent societal pressure to make families of their own. They see their friends spitting out kids and marrying great Provider men with high social status, and dammit, they deserve the same thing!

Some women (not all) are so desperate for the life they *"deserve,"* they will have no hesitation about lying and manipulating to achieve it.

BE MORE LIKE A WOMAN

I've said it again and again: Men are the romantics in relationships. They truly believe that women will love them solely for their personality, soul, kindness and good-heartedness. Many men refuse to believe that while their wives DO truly love them, it absolutely is a CONDITIONAL love (as it should be). She's not your mother, after all. She's your romantic partner. There ARE conditions that can lead to the shut-down of the relationship. Unfortunately, the conditions are sometimes WAY simpler than what many men want to acknowledge. We always assume since we don't emotionally/physically abuse or neglect our spouses in any way that everything is good to go. We think our sweet nature keeps the evil temptations away from our relationships.

Wives have a checklist for actors in the husband/father role of their life movies. If one or more of their needs on the checklist aren't routinely being met, their *"must procure new mate"* behavior switch is flipped, and the *"detaching from my husband"* machine cranks away. They'll be looking for a new actor to fill the role in no time at all. Many men will throw their hands up in disgust and see this as an example of typical female fickleness ruining a perfectly good life-long relationship. Yes, it's true that women are more emotion-driven and have certain behavioral tendencies and personality traits like higher rates of neuroticism, but when it comes to choosing a mate to partner with for life, they can be pragmatic in their approach. Many men who have lost their jobs or became physically injured quickly discovered just how disloyal and cruel their wives can be under the right circumstances.

I always tell men they must TRY to exercise their rational brain muscle and be more like women in relationships, specifically when it comes to choosing and maintaining a relationship with another person. We must be steadfast and strong and keep our eyes and ears open for the bad things that can not only bring down our relationships but also ruin our lives completely. We must develop our own list of *"must haves"* for a partner and STICK TO IT no matter what. We must be as cold and calculating as the fairer sex has no fear of being.

While she may say, *"Oh, you lost your job? I don't think this is going to work out,"* you are also free to say, *"Oh, you have been diagnosed with depression and borderline personality disorder... I don't think this will work for me,"* or, *"I see you are unemployed and have two kids already. No thanks! Not interested!"* Stop putting women on a pedestal and realize that they are flawed human beings and may not be a good match for you. Don't be afraid to put your needs first. Be the bad guy. Be the asshole. Look past her intoxicating feminine charms and see her for what she may be: A flawed human being who can flush you and everything you love down the toilet.

I know... easier said than done. It's so very tough not to get washed away by the hormones and feel-good chemicals that overwhelm our brains in the presence of a woman, especially one that seems to be so physically and emotionally compatible with you. As they say, when you have the rose-colored glasses on, all the red flags just look like flags. You won't be the first man fooled by the sweet siren song of a beautiful woman, and you certainly won't be the last. It's just part of the game. You need to learn the rules of this game, or you WILL lose.

NEEDINESS AND SOCIAL ANXIETY

If there is one thing you need to eliminate TODAY from your single dating persona, it is your neediness. Yes, you are probably a needy person. We all are, to some degree. If you're a recently cheated-on divorced guy who just wants to be loved… your neediness is probably through the roof and immediately apparent to everyone in your social circle. For your platonic friends and potential romantic partners, it is absolutely a HUGE turnoff. Nothing is more of a repellant than male behavior that says, *"I NEED you, your attention, your love, and your affection."* There's a whole collection of awful behavior that comes with neediness, and people just naturally shy away from it. Unless, of course, the other person is mentally ill or severely broken themselves, then they FEED upon your neediness like a pit bull on a steak. This is precisely why super nice guys always seem to attract the biggest psychos.

Thanks to the growing normalcy of broken families and abusive childhoods, you can't swing a dead cat without hitting a woman with abandonment issues or full-blown borderline personality disorder. These women NEED to be NEEDED and they latch on to broken men like an alien face-hugger. When you put forward your Provider qualities hoping to snag a mate, you are inherently advertising your neediness. You are putting up a giant neon sign that says, *"Broken? Nobody else will touch you with a ten-foot pole? Tired of jumping from man to man? Look no further! I'm your knight in shining armor! I will look right past all your glaring faults! Plus… I have stuff I will gladly give you! Money! Time! Lots of love and affection! What are you waiting for?! Please, just give me a chance."* Mentally ill women that are completely ignored by the MHNNM will flock to you, and then discard you like a used napkin.

SOCIAL ANXIETY

A good number of men that are fresh out of a divorce try to throw themselves out there in the dating world, and quickly report back just how much of a stressful and negative emotional experience it was. To quote a reader from my Facebook group:

"Was with the ex for twenty years, since we were sixteen, and she was my only sexual partner. I'm hoping to experience some good stuff going forward. Just feel so socially awkward and anxious around people. Was at my first ever singles night last week and hated it. Hardly spoke to anyone and convinced myself I'd be alone forever."

What is happening for guys like this reader is one of two things:

1. They realize that they've always been anxious around other people. They've been effectively hiding in the cocoon of their marriages all these years, using their wives as a psychological crutch and outlet for their emotions and vulnerabilities that they don't feel comfortable sharing with the rest of the world. They never really put themselves out there before, so they have no way of coping with the anxiety that comes with meeting new people. In the reader's case above, he jumped right into the deep end of the pool (a singles night), became terrified, ashamed of his reaction, and later questioned his worth as a future romantic partner.

2. They used to be outgoing and personable guys, but the trauma of divorce left an emotional wound that is still healing. These men are shocked at how going out to meet new people (something they used to be good at), or even something as simple as seeing a photo of a friend and their loving family is enough to trigger anxiety or even a full-blown panic attack. Men underestimate their brokenness and attempt to overcome the obvious with false bravado and ego-driven stupidity. These guys just need to learn to walk again before they even think about running a marathon.

Most of the guys I talk to fall into one of the above two categories. Both need to take a time out, forget about jumping into the scary bottomless ocean, and instead go take some basic swimming lessons. They need to take very real and deliberate baby steps towards becoming a more centered and confident social person again. When you're a broken dude, people (especially women) can smell it a mile away. You may try to convince yourself that you're ready to jump in, but you'll end up breathing in water, panicking, and the lifeguard will have to jump in to save you. You'll be embarrassed and everyone will now see you as *"that guy that almost died."* Not good.

Being social, like anything else, is a skill. It takes practice.

It means being brave. It means being vulnerable around strangers. You achieve that state of social Zen by gaining little wins along the way. How to start? Very simple. I like the plan of forcing yourself to talk to at least five people every day. Small talk, as we say in America. Nothing serious. You're not hitting on a girl. You're not trying to make best friends with some random guy. You're just putting yourself out there and saying, *"Hi. You don't know me… but here's something a little positive for you."*

Some ideas:

1. To some random guy at a parking lot, *"Dude. I love your car. What year is it? Very nice choice. Have a good one!"*

2. To some woman on an elevator, *"Those are some pretty snazzy boots. I like the leather. Very cool. Later!"*

3. To your waitress, *"Oh, the breakfast was very good. Thank you, Nancy. Don't work too hard today. Have a good one!"*

4. To a guy at work, *"Hey, thanks for that thing you did the other day. Much appreciated. I'm heading to the coffee shop. Want something? It's on me."*

5. To the old lady at the grocery store, *"Ma'am, you need some help with that? Looks like a lot to carry."*

Little positive steps. Makes the other person's day a little brighter. Makes you feel a little more positive, and with every interaction, a little braver and more confident. These quick positive interactions aren't anything like the stupid singles event. At the singles event, you're just fumbling with your drink and staring at your shoes, trying to get up the nerve to talk to the pretty brunette across the room. The reason that scenario is so stressful is because of the understood dynamic at play. You're looking for a mate, and so is she. That naturally means you're in a contest to win her over. You're competing with the dozens of other guys trying to get the hot girl's attention. Right away, the scenario is one of competition and pressure. She's judging you from the moment you step into the room. She may have made up her mind about you already, without saying a word to each other. Overall, it's just a bad scene for a socially awkward dude. You're introducing an unnecessarily high level of anxiety for absolutely no reason. If a singles function is your barometer for how you are doing socially, then you'll just fail and push yourself further into isolation and eventual depression.

You need little wins. The little wins build momentum. That's how you crawl out of your social anxiety hole. You do so by opening yourself up to people, making yourself a little vulnerable, adding a little something positive to the other person's day, and then backing off. The key to why these interactions are so genuine and effective is that there is no understood reciprocity at work. You just made them feel good, and you wanted nothing from them in return. With the singles event, there is always an expectation of return. If the woman agrees to talk to you, she is opening herself up to the very real possibility of being asked out, going on a horrible date, having to deal with a guy she realizes that she really doesn't like, turning him down for future dates, dealing with his emotions, etc. She has to give up much of her time and energy to a probable lost cause and negative result. To her, talking to some random nervous guy at a singles mixer is a big freaking deal. You, the nervous guy, already have two strikes against you before you even step up to the plate.

The singles mixer, online dating, meeting your friend's sister who recently got divorced… these all require next-level social skills to navigate successfully. If you find yourself anxious around people, you need to get a lot of practice in before you jump into the deep end of the socializing pool.

ABUNDANCE

If there's one thing that harms a great deal of men in all facets of life, it's a feeling of *"scarcity."* In short, many men feel that good stuff in life is in such short supply (especially for themselves), that they have to hang on to whatever crumb of positivity they can get. This feeling of scarcity permeates everything about them, their jobs, their friendships, and yes, their romantic relationships.

The opposite of scarcity is *"abundance."* When you have a feeling of abundance in life, you have a feeling that your own personal worth as a human being is such that you naturally create and attract positive things. You don't *"settle"* for substandard. You never say, *"I better shut up. I'm lucky to have this."* You don't tolerate awfulness and abuse from a person because they USED to be really nice to you and you hope to one day get that person back into your life. Your sense of worth is way too high for such nonsense.

Let's look at some realistic examples of scarcity and abundance in action:

Frank is hired at a new job. During the interview process, he was told up front he would not have to work weekends. *"Good,"* he told the boss. *"I need to be with my kids over the weekends, so that is great to hear."* A whopping two weeks into the job, he is called into the boss' office. *"I'm going to need you to come in Saturday and work all day. All weekend, really. It's all hands on deck. We have to get this project done by Monday. No excuses."* Frank walks out of the office in an angry and confused daze. He knows what the boss said before, but now he feels obligated to come in over the weekend. *"Sigh… now I need to see if my ex can take the kids this weekend. Maybe my mom can watch them."*

Frank goes into the office over the weekend and expects to see cubicles filled with people furiously working away. After several hours, it is clear… it's only going to be him, the boss, and one other guy. *"Where's Dave?"* Frank asks his coworker. *"Oh, he had some soccer tournament out of state he had to go to."* *"What the hell?! I thought it was all hands on deck!?"* Frank says. His friend laughs. *"Yeah, well… so did I."*

After that weekend, Frank is now pegged as being *"the guy you ask to do extra stuff and take up the slack for others."* While this may sound like a great way to get ahead in a company, Frank later learns that it's just a great way to work double the hours for the same pay as the other guy. What Frank doesn't see is that Dave was approached months ago by the same boss with the same *"work on weekends"* request. The only difference is that Dave politely said no. *"Family comes first."* Instead of fighting with Dave and getting his employment agreement thrown in his face, the boss does what every boss in this situation does: He looks for the next victim. That next victim was Frank. Now that Frank showed his weakness, the boss won't let up. It won't be his last weekend request.

Frank has a very real sense of scarcity when it comes to jobs. If you were to press him on the matter, you may hear that he has a fear of conflict, doesn't want to be an asshole, doesn't want to let his team down, etc. The real reason is he doesn't want to lose his damn job. He's lucky to have it. If he rocks the boat, he could get fired! His coworker Dave, on the other hand, knows that he has worth. He knows he puts in good hours and gets the job done. The boss is lucky to have somebody like him Monday through Friday. The boss better not push his luck with the weekend requests, or else he'll take his skills to the competition. When it comes to jobs, Dave has a sense of abundance.

Jim finally meets the girl of his dreams. She is drop-dead gorgeous. A real head-turner. They have a three-month honeymoon phase where everything is perfect and amazing. He can't believe his luck. Then the wheels fall off the relationship. His girlfriend, Stacy, screams at him in front of his friends… all because he spilled a drink. She gets belligerent when he doesn't answer her text messages right away. *"Are you cheating on me?!"* She starts openly flirting and texting other men. When Jim expresses displeasure with this, she becomes infuriated. *"You can't tell me not to talk to my friends!"*

Jim hangs on for dear life in the relationship as Stacy seems to do everything to push him away. Why? *"I mean, dude, look at her? Are you serious? I'm lucky to have a girl like that. She's a once-in-a-lifetime kind of girlfriend."*

Jim has a very real sense of scarcity when it comes to girls. Now that he has a pretty one, he hangs on for dear life. Even when she does everything that falls under the category of *"crazy ex-girlfriend,"* Jim feels like he can't let go. He feels *that after this relationship is over*, he'll go the rest of his life with substandard women, or worse… alone.

Jim's friend Todd has very real abundance when it comes to women. It's not like he's been with dozens of women in his life, but he values his time on the planet enough to know that he can't waste a minute on a "crazy" girlfriend. As soon as he sees the warning signs, he *pulls the* ejection handle on the relationship. His friends call him *"ruthless"* when it comes to breaking up with girls. He often tells the story of the time a girl lied to him about smoking. She knew he thought smoking was gross. One evening, he found cigarettes hidden in her bathroom and he immediately left and told her they were over. This was right before he was about to have sex with the woman! She was laying on the bed wearing sexy lingerie that he bought her with her legs open and waiting for him. He just walked out of the bathroom, threw the packet of cigarettes at her, and said, *"You lied. We're done."*

Todd's friends always try to get him to share the story of the sexy smoker chick at all their gatherings. *"Dude, you could've at least banged her before you left! That chick was a smoke show!"* "Nope," Todd says, *"it wasn't worth the drama. I don't like liars and I fucking hate smoking."* Todd has abundance when it comes to women. He has integrity, as well. He knows what he will and will not tolerate. He has lines that cannot be crossed… if even the woman is hot, spread eagled in bed, and wearing sexy lingerie. Besides, that woman is one of a million women that Todd could be with. He has a very real sense of abundance when it comes to women in his life… and that has kept him out of a lot of trouble.

THE SECRET TO PICKING UP WOMEN

There are a lot of expert *"Pickup Artist"* men out there that are willing to take a lot of your money to show you how best to attract women. Many socially awkward nice guys from all over the world regularly fork over thousands of bucks to go to boot camps and seminars run by former nerdy men who claim to have the secrets to unlocking physical and emotional intimacy from hot women. These programs are a mixture of human behavior study, evolutionary psychology, and motivational speaking. You can probably learn 99% of what they teach by doing YouTube searches and watching videos for a few days. These Pickup Artists are simply nerdy guys who sat back and watched the successful Lover guys and broke down their behaviors into digestible chunks of actionable behavior.

Allow me to save you a lot of time and money. I'll break down the secrets for you:

1. Be attractive.
2. Be fun. Be different.
3. Be confident and aware of your value.

There… that's it. You're welcome. Now, let's break it down a little further.

1. BE ATTRACTIVE

Yes, it's important that you look good. Very important. Can't overstate it. I'm amazed at how many men don't realize how they LOOK has a great deal to do with why their ex-wives never seemed to want to have sex with them or why they can't seem to get women to return their messages. We're all animals, after all. We are all looking for certain indicators of physical health and virility. For women, they're looking for indicators of health, virility and strength. Yes, they like muscles. I don't care what they tell you, they like muscles. They may not like giant balloon bodybuilder muscles. They may not like huge fat strongman muscles… but they like a guy who looks good in a t-shirt. They like a lean, mean fighting machine. They like a guy who can take care of himself AND take care of her in case things go sideways in a hurry. They want to grab on to an arm or put a hand on your chest and feel something solid. They like a manly man.

They also like a man who looks like he cares about his appearance. They like a guy who keeps up with the fashion trends and doesn't look like he's stuck in the eighties. Put the jean shorts and white dad sneakers away. Get on a program like Stitch Fix or Menlo House that will send you hip and current clothing on a monthly basis. Basically, just act like you care about what you wear. Put some thought into it. How you decide to show yourself to the world is very important. Whether it's at the office, at the job site, at the singles bar… your clothes say it all. What are you saying? Are you saying, *"I'm a comfortable dad,"* or are you saying, *"I'm fun and different from all the other guys my age. I'm actually pretty cool and interesting*"? The choice is yours.

2. BE FUN — BE DIFFERENT

"So, what do you like to do for fun?" This is the quintessential dating icebreaker for single women. What they are saying: *"So, tell me what life with you would be like."* If somebody today asks me that, I would say that I love working out, playing basketball, reading, writing, watching movies, going to sports games, art, playing guitar, and traveling to places like NYC, New Orleans, California, Costa Rica, Canada and Europe… oh, and I just started learning how to ski. That paints a pretty good picture of exactly WHO I am as a potential date. What if I said, *"I like fantasy football, craft beer, and golf"*? That says, *"I do what every other guy out there does. There is absolutely NOTHING unique about me. Not a shred of mystery or fun here."* Zzzzzzzz.

Be fun. Be different. Be INTERESTING. Stick out from the crowd. Think of what your dream date would say after spending a weekend with you. She's having coffee with her best friends, and they ask, *"Soooo? How was the date with that guy you met online? What's he like?"* What's she going to say? *"Oh, he's nice. He has kids. Really good guy."* That's it? Wow. Before she can finish the sentence, she is thinking, *"Alright… maybe he's not that great after all. I'm wasting my time."* Remember, your dream date is a mentally healthy woman. That means she's got her shit together. She's not looking for a rock-solid father figure in her life. She's not looking for the guy who won't go anywhere when she acts crazy and breaks his stuff in a fit of rage. She's looking for the good guy that will be fun to be with. She's looking for the sexy diversion from her stressful life. Be THAT guy.

3. KNOW YOUR VALUE

If there's one thing that brings down a good man in dating, it's the deep-down feeling that he is just not that great of a catch. His lack of self-worth makes it so that any attention he gets from women is to be cherished and held on to as long as humanly possible. He feels like he is LUCKY to get a reply from a text he sends to a girl he met online. He is LUCKY to get a date with her. He is LUCKY to get a kiss from her. Never in the nice guy's wildest dreams does he think that SHE is lucky to be in HIS presence. This state of mind permeates everything about his persona. Like sharks being able to smell a drop of blood a mile away, dangerous women can smell low self-esteem from something simple like your frequent text messages and self-deprecating humor.

You must always keep in mind that there are literally about one hundred thousand women that you are compatible with, and they would date you and have a great time (assuming you have your shit together and are a man of value). I'm not going to tell you the typical *"There are million women out there for you!"* nonsense. Given geographical limitations, time, etc., it's not THAT big a pool of candidates, but it is a huge number that you're never going to exhaust. Trust me. The women are out there. Lots of them.

Just the simple act of KNOWING that you have value and

options in life already puts you above many men in the male dating pool. If you're out on a date with a woman and she instantly starts acting horribly and bluntly states that she's tired of dating losers who don't pay for everything… you can simply smile, shake her hand and say, *"Ha. I tell you what… I don't think this is going to work out."* Then you walk away. You keep your self-respect, you save yourself from hours, days, months and possibly years of anguish at the hands of an awful woman… and you further set yourself apart from the crowd. Watch as the formerly angry woman eventually sends you text messages apologizing for her behavior. She was in a bad mood. Work was terrible that day. She got into an argument with her sister. She was just not on her A game, and she would like another chance. All of that may be true, but there's another side to the story: You passed her test. Yes, it was a test. She threw a proverbial punch at your face (her bitchy attitude), and you ducked and countered with a right jab to her nose (your willingness to immediately walk away and forget her). You didn't stand there and take blow after blow from her. You're too tough and smart for that. You passed her test.

WOMEN TEST MEN, CONSTANTLY

If you sit back and watch people like I do, you notice certain behavioral dynamics come up again and again. Watch a single man and a single woman who are obviously attracted to each other meet for the first time at a party. They do the normal greetings we all do. He smiles to show he's healthy and has all his pearly white choppers. She shakes his hand… but not too roughly. She wants to come across as weak and submissive to his tougher masculine persona. She doesn't want to damage his fragile male ego. He sucks in his stomach to appear thinner. She twirls her hair and blushes slightly, both universal signs of arousal. Her red lipstick and makeup further give the impression of flushed skin. Yes, it's all one big, predictable, hilarious, animalistic mating ritual.

Everything seems to go well with the small talk, and then the woman decides, perhaps unconsciously, to kick things up a notch. Almost out of nowhere, she will throw a test at him. This is commonly in the form of a very slight (or not so slight) insult. This may be some little verbal jab at an obvious fault of his (like his height or his age). Maybe she takes a piece of information the man just gave her and spins it around to make him look bad. *"My ex used to ride motorcycles, too. I have always thought of it as just a stupid mid-life crisis. There are so many other more worthwhile things to do if you want to enjoy life."*

With these female tests, there are a few ways to react:

1. **Explain, qualify, and apologize.** In the case of the woman insulting his motorcycle hobby, the man may say, *"Yeah, I can totally see how you may think that. A lot of guys are poser dorks on the motorcycles. Lots of bored doctors and lawyers with too much money pretending to be bikers. I'm not like that at all, though. I take it seriously. I dunno... I mean... maybe one day I'll grow tired of it and take up golf. Probably not a bad idea. Playing outlaw biker guy gets old after a while. My mom freaks out every time go for a ride. She's worried sick I will get in an accident. Hasn't happened yet,*

knock on wood."

With this reaction, the man just took his life's passion and completely threw it under the bus... all to appease the pretty woman he just met ten minutes ago. He instantly tried to explain and qualify himself by making fun of other men. This is a common ploy. *"I'm not like those OTHER guys!"* Then he brought up his mom, for some strange reason. Total swing and a miss. Instant loss of respect. She doesn't know why exactly, but she suddenly wants to go back and talk to that other guy she met earlier in the evening.

2. **Be insulted.** *"Well, who asked you for your opinion, anyway? You know what, you're not all that like you think you are. I'm wasting my time talking to you. Later."* If you're genuinely insulted and have no interest in the woman, this is certainly one direction to go in. Take what she says seriously, let her know she angered you, and bail on the conversation. Keep in mind that what you feel may be a manly and *"take no bullshit"* way to walk away with your dignity may be seen by her and others as a major hissy fit from an overly sensitive guy who lets a strange woman too easily dictate his mood. She played you like a puppet.

3. **Be playful and confident.** *"Well, I was deeply involved in the world of male jello wrestling for many years, but I pulled a hamstring. Had to forfeit my championship belt. I got bored, and I figured riding a bike was the next best thing. Don't get me wrong, I still break out the jello and baby pool occasionally. You know, family BBQs and stuff."* This reaction not only says, *"I have a sense of humor and don't take myself too*

seriously," but it also shows that you are NOT affected on an emotional level by the random snotty comment by some gal you just met. Yes, she's pretty, but she's also just another human you met at a party. Big F'ing deal if she thinks bikes are stupid. She's not the Queen, and even if she was… you still wouldn't give a shit.

Yes, the female tests are very real, and they extend WAY beyond the dating phase of a relationship. Wives test their men up until the moment they're put in the ground (and probably after). Women have an innate need to measure and qualify important men in their life. The overall goal is to determine if you are worthy of their respect and their time. Respect and time are very limited in the woman's world, and she can't mess around with somebody who will waste both (another way we could learn a thing or two from women). If you appear to be a really great guy, you're attractive enough, and you click on an emotional level, BUT you immediately cave in to one little jab she throws your way, then you're immediately discarded and put in the *"maybe I will date him when I need to talk and have a free meal"* pile… and for good reason: You're weak. You ain't ready for the dating game, and you're not worth her time.

A lot of men catch on to the tests that women put them through and will proudly proclaim that these are just GAMES women play, and they (as rational manly men) don't play games. Men like to feel that they are above the silly and shallow behavior that they see women putting men through. To that, I say:

"The game is going on whether you are playing or not. The entire mating ritual and subsequent relationship is one giant game."

From the moment you get up the nerve to approach the girl, to the birth of your first child, to the time you both retire, to the moment you take your last breath… the woman in your life is going to test the shit out of you. You may call it nagging, being a bitch, playing games, not saying what she really means, being deceitful, being manipulative, etc.… but it doesn't change the fact that it's all going on and it will absolutely continue to go on. You must recognize when the tests happen and know how to deal with them.

Here are some of the most common tests given by women in relationships:

ASKING YOU TO MAKE A DECISION

This is one that is the subject of countless internet memes and comedy routines. Wife says she is hungry. "Where do you want to go eat?" the husband asks. *"I don't know,"* the wife says. Husband suggests Chinese food. Wife says no. Husband suggests pizza. Wife says no. And so on and so on.… Husband gets frustrated. *"Just tell me what you feel like!"* For some reason, this makes the wife even more angry and frustrated. Husband interprets this as typical female indecision and a strange desire to make drama and chaos from something as innocuous as deciding where to go eat.

In this situation, the ideal (but rare) male response would

be to say, *"Sweet. We're going for pizza. You have ten minutes to get ready, Ms. Sexy Pants. If not ready by then, I'm going without you."* Wife may pout and act offended at his abrasive attitude, but in the end, she will probably grab her stuff and go along and enjoy some pizza and have a little more respect for the man who can take charge and handle something as simple as where to go eat. Worst case is that she REALLY didn't feel like pizza that night and she will be a little more assertive next time and give her man some better direction. Win/Win. Respect and better communication in the end.

The question of where to eat sounds silly, but it really is an excellent test of your ability to lead and make a decision and relieve her of that day-to-day stress that eats away at her attraction towards you. Simply put, indecisiveness on the part of the man is a sign of weakness. It means, *"Please don't give me the stress of making a decision. Please relieve me of this burden, oh mentally stronger woman in my life,"* or even worse, *"I'm afraid to give direction right now because I know you will just disagree with me and that makes me feel stressed and I can't take it so please just decide for us so that I know you are happy."* Both are NOT good and both result in a loss of respect.

"I SAW YOU LOOKING AT THAT GIRL. DO YOU THINK SHE IS CUTE?"

So many men cave into this test and approach it the wrong way. Remember, as I said in chapter two *"Why Did This Happen?"* a woman's sexual attraction towards you depends on several factors, one of which is your ability to attract other women. If other women find you desirable, then your value as a partner just shot through the roof. If your woman flat out asks you if you find that other woman attractive, she's asking you if you are still an honest sexual being. Do you still have your very real and very normal sex drive that every healthy man should have? Are you willing to put up with your woman's possible shitty response and tell her the truth, or are you going to lie and tell her you have zero attraction towards other obviously hot women to appease your woman's low self-esteem in that moment?

The right answer is a form of playful honesty. *"Yeah, she's not bad. I sure wouldn't kick her out of bed,"* or, *"What? I'm sorry, I didn't hear what you said. I was fantasizing about life with that nineteen-year-old that just walked past us."* These responses show you are honest and playful, but also that a pretty girl walking by and getting your attention is no big deal. It happens all the time. Nothing to freak out about. What you don't do is explain away and tell her that no other woman exists and that she is crazy for thinking you are staring at some obviously pretty girl. Of course you were staring. Your WOMAN was staring. Everyone in the vicinity was staring. It was a pretty girl. That's like saying, *"DON'T STARE AT THE BEAUTIFUL SUNSET!"* You're going to stare. It's completely natural. So, man up and be honest. Deal with the subsequent hissy fit from your woman, and deal with the long-term positive repercussions of a woman who respects you a little more for being an honest man with a healthy libido.

"ARE YOU SAYING YOU'D RATHER GO OUT WITH YOUR FRIENDS INSTEAD OF BEING WITH ME?"

As men, we like to get away from women on a regular basis and recalibrate our sense of self. We like our time with our buddies or time to ourselves to be alone. This is normal and healthy. This is why guys like to go to the garage to tinker with the car, escape to the *"man cave"* to play some guitar, hang out and play poker with the boys, etc. All of those things do NOT involve the women in our lives. It keeps us mentally balanced. This is an understood part of being a man and one a sane and healthy partner would recognize and support.

When your woman has a fit of low self-esteem or anxiety about your relationship and asks, *"What… you don't want to be with me on Saturday? You'd rather go hang out with Dave and drink beer and watch football?"* she is seeing if you NEED her (neediness is not good) and will chicken out and cave in to her emotions (fear of her is not good). The answer from any man should be, *"Yes, of course. I enjoy time with my friends. It's good for me. See you later tonight. Love you, babe."* If your woman takes great offense to this and you honestly feel that she always NEEDS to be with you, then you should probably question the long-term viability of your relationship. She is exhibiting an inability to cope with the stress of being alone and may have a genuine fear of abandonment. These are two signs that your world is about to go right down the shitter in a hurry. You've been warned.

"PLEASE PUT UP A BOUNDARY FOR ME AND SAVE ME FROM MY OWN BAD DECISION-MAKING."

I saved the best for last. As far as common woman tests are concerned, this is the one that is one of the most insidious. Your wife may very well be right at the edge of crossing the line into inappropriate behavior territory, and she has either consciously or subconsciously reached out to you for help. She wants you to play the bad guy, figuratively smack her on the behind and say, *"No! Bad girl!"*

An example of this may be, *"Do you feel bad when I go out drinking with my friends on Fridays? I know I've been out the past three weeks and left you with the kids. I don't want you to be mad."* So many men respond to this in the completely wrong way. *"No! Baby, seriously. Go out and have fun! I love when you enjoy yourself. The kids and I are fine."* Usually, the man is NOT fine with such an arrangement, but he doesn't want to rock the boat and have a pissy wife sitting at home pouting on a Friday. Plus, his nice guy ways make him recoil at the thought of playing the part of the bad guy. He always wants to be Mr. Agreeable Guy. In his mind, that's the more secure and honorable method of being a husband.

Even if the man were in fact completely okay with his wife going out on the town four Fridays in a row (maybe he likes the time alone to mentally recalibrate), the mere act of his wife bringing it up and asking his opinion should cause his gut to question the reality of the situation. Why is she asking him this now? Probably because she recognizes that her behavior is coming close to crossing the line, and she's a little scared of what may happen next… yet she, for whatever reason, feels powerless to stop it herself. Maybe she heavily flirted with several guys at the dance club last week and can't wait to go back and do it again. Maybe she drank way too much and got sick and felt like a terrible mom, yet she can't imagine a boring Friday at home with her husband and kids. Whatever the case may be, by approaching the man and saying, *"Are you SURE this is okay with you?"* she's saying, *"Please show me you're invested enough in us as a couple that you don't mind playing the bad guy and telling me to act like a responsible adult."* When the man says, *"No, everything is cool,"* the wife's internal response is, *"Oh well. I tried. I guess he doesn't care."*

Show her you care. Show her you don't mind playing the part of the bad guy. Show her you don't mind the inevitable fit that will come your way. You are in the relationship for the long haul, and many times that means playing a paternal role that many men just aren't comfortable with. As with all these tests, show her you don't mind putting on the captain's uniform and leading. There's nothing sexier than a man in a uniform, even if it's a metaphorical one.

THE DELICATE BALANCING GAME

Let's face it, being in a relationship is being a man on hard mode. It's a constant struggle to maintain your independence, compromise when appropriate, validate, be sensitive, be vulnerable, be tough, be stoic, be honest, be true to your sexuality… all at the same time. It's learning when you're being tested, when you need to apologize, and when you just need to shut the hell up and walk away from the situation temporarily… or maybe even permanently.

The walk away part is toughest for nice guys. Broken women that are in relationships with nice guys understand this better than anyone. They know they can get away with murder. If you give them an inch, they will absolutely take a mile. They can say and do what they want with impunity. These are the women that will kick a man when he is down. They recognize they can push and cross over boundaries regularly and the nice guy will always give them the benefit of the doubt. The MHNNM always has the *"walk away forever"* card in his back pocket, and he's not afraid to use it. He's not afraid to be the biggest asshole on the planet Earth for the few minutes it takes to say, *"I think I'm done with us. I appreciate all you've done, but this is over."*

The winner in all relationships (professional, romantic, etc.) is the one that has the least to lose. He or she can walk away and say, *"It's cool. No biggy. Have a great life."* The loser is the one that absolutely NEEDS the relationship to continue or else their whole life falls apart. The users and manipulators pick up on this NEED and take full advantage of it. The guy at the office who has no backbone, no marketable skills, and no other job prospects is asked again and again to come in on weekends and stay late to finish up some projects. The guy who knows how to play office politics and has a good network of professional connections gets to play golf and drink beers with the boss instead. He knows how to play the game. He found the right balance for the relationship.

A man needs to find the right balance between nice/sensitive and tough/stoic for his romantic relationships. You have to wear both the Lover and the Provider hats. Many men fresh out of poor relationships will recognize that they stayed way too long on the nice/sensitive (Provider) side of the fence and watched as it slowly eroded away at the health of their relationships. In response, their post-relationship selves will swing that pendulum all the way over to the other side and attempt to become super alpha male tough guy. He's the one that can be heard saying, *"All women are whores,"* after a few beers with his buddies. He's the one that will stomp his feet and yell, *"Well, fuck you, you slut!"* after being turned down by a woman at the dance club. He's simply pissed that he's not invited to the fun relationship party. He thought he played by the rules (by being a nice guy) and life didn't reward him as he thought it should. So, he tries out Plan B: Embracing his asshole side. What a lot of guys unfortunately realize is that there are many women out there who actually DO prefer being intimate with a selfish, mean asshole over a pushover nice guy. If the former nice

guy turns into an asshole and starts getting laid a lot more…
he's going to remain an asshole for a while. In fact, he may
even turn the asshole dial up a few notches. As far as he's
concerned, it works. Then he gets hurt and he goes back to
being the nice guy again.

The secret, like all things in life, is in the middle ground.
It's remaining stoic in your approach to stress that life (and
your woman) throws at you, being a ruthless bastard when
you need to be, and randomly doing nice things for your
woman just because you love her to death, and you want
her to feel appreciated for all that she does for you and your
family. It's also being willing and able to play the part of the
ultimate bad guy and walking away from it all when the
negatives far outweigh the positives.

IS THE JUICE WORTH THE SQUEEZE?

There's a time in every relationship when a man looks at
the constant struggle of maintaining the delicate balance
of Lover/Provider and he asks himself, *"Is it worth it?"* Is
dealing with her constant tests and nagging worth the once-
a-week great sex and close friendship? Is her beautiful smile
and fantastic backside enough to overcome her near constant fits of angry jealousy? Do her exceptional qualities as a
mom and friend overcome her expanding waistline and her
lack of sex drive? Does he grow tired of having to constantly
play the paternal role and keeping his wife from crossing
the line into inappropriate behavior territory? Does he just
wish she would grow up and stop being so damn emotional
half the time?

*"Show me the hottest woman on the planet, and I'll show you
a guy that is sick of her shit."*

For the MHNNM who is trying out a monogamous relationship, his patience may be razor thin. After all, he recognizes the abundance of casual relationship candidates that
are out there, he recognizes his value as a mate, the value of
his time, and he recognizes the potential danger involved
with some of the glaring red flags that others would simply
write off as *"typical girlfriend behavior."*

To the MHNNM, having a casual girlfriend who constantly questions his whereabouts is not worth the hassle. He
knows potentially dangerous abandonment issues when
he sees them. A woman who always seems to try to make
him jealous will be dropped quicker than she can say, "A
cute guy at the gym today said I was really hot and wanted
my number." The MHNNM recognizes unhealthy atten-
tion-seeking habits. He just has no time or patience for the
silliness. Could he be dropping genuinely good long-term
relationship candidates by bailing out so quickly? Is he far
too impatient? Maybe. Maybe not. Again, the MHNNM
doesn't NEED a long-term relationship to function, so he
can afford to let a good one slip through the cracks if that
means dropping twelve other psychos that could ruin the
life he has worked so hard for. Ironically, his willingness
to hit the eject button makes him way more attractive.
Remember, women want what they can't have. If he's not
chasing, then his value must be high.

For some men in long-term relationships, these *"Is it all worth it?"* questions are eventually answered for them when they have an affair with the cute twenty-year-old from work and leave their wives and families. That's the easy and chickenshit way out of a difficult situation. They hit the restart button with a new, fresh face and ride off into the sunset as the intense high of the new relationship floods their brains. As a guy once told me years ago, *"Man... there ain't nothing better in the world than new pussy."* The man who runs off with his new girlfriend will eventually just do the whole long relationship process all over again. First, the new relationship energy with tons of sex. Then the familiarity. Back to boredom. Back to drama. Then resignation. Rince and repeat.

For most men, however, they linger in a state of relationship limbo for years. They're not quite happy with several parts of the relationship, but they convince themselves that they are happy enough with the other parts. They make do with what they have. They don't want to rock the boat and potentially ruin the whole marriage just because they're not happy with several huge negative things their wives do on a regular basis.

For the nice guy that avoids confrontation and just *"lets it go,"* he's actually telling his wife that their relationship isn't worth the hard work needed to make it better. More specifically, SHE isn't worth the hard work. SHE isn't worth being honest with and telling her when she is doing something that is slowly but surely eating away at his attraction to her. Instead, the nice guy will put up with his wife's negative actions and ignore and occasionally physically and mentally escape from his wife. The wife will eventually pick up on his growing resentment. She may see that he is becoming more distant and disconnected from her and ask him what is wrong. The man, on the other hand, feels that his wife should just KNOW when she's doing something wrong. He shouldn't HAVE to tell her (a very feminine quality of the nice guy). Eventually, the resentment and anger may boil over, usually at a very stressful time, and the husband blows up at the wife. The wife sits back and listens. Instead of apologizing or empathizing with her husband's feelings, she's overwhelmed by her disgust with him in that moment. Why? Because he had issues with her over all these months/years, and he was too scared to tell her. *"Wow... what kind of man is he?"* All of this drama could've been avoided if the man took a chance months or years ago and said, *"Stop. What you're doing right now is not good. I don't like it."* When he finally blows his top, the wife's subsequent lack of empathy and remorse is baffling and further infuriating to the man. The resentment continues to build for both part-ners.

Once you are in a committed relationship with a woman, decide if the inevitable hard work of keeping the relation-ship machine running is really worth the time and effort. If you see so many red flags and your foreseeable future is filled with abuse or unnecessary stress, then you need to take the next step and do what is right for both you and her. End the relationship. But, before doing so, ask yourself what part YOU played in bringing about the current situa-tion. Did you do all you could to improve yourself and the relationship? Have you really been the captain of the ship and played the role necessary to keep the boat afloat? Have you truly stepped up and been the fearless asshole that you sometimes need to be? More often than not, the answer is no. Live and learn.

Your current relationship may be over for good, but you need to take the right energy and the right mindset into your future. If you're like most men I work with, you will end up with another woman… probably sooner than you realize. The rush of positive energy that a seemingly *"perfect"* woman brings to your world is beyond intoxicating. Before you know it, your bank account is drained, you're taking care of somebody else's kid, and you're wondering why it burns when you pee.

Be very careful.

PHIL'S STORY

Phil went through the hell of divorce and came out on the other side looking pretty good. He lost a great deal of money, but the time spent away from his toxic ex and the stress of their marriage opened his eyes and his brain to many more professional possibilities. His career flourished. His health improved, as well. His anxiety-fueled weight loss gave him momentum to hit the gym, eat right, and look better than he ever had in his life.

About three months after his divorce, Phil met somebody he thought was very special. It was a friend of a friend. Her name was Candy. What Phil didn't know was that his chance meeting with Candy wasn't so random. His friends knowingly put them both in a position to meet at a Christmas party. She was recently divorced, as well. As Phil would later learn, she fit the mold of what everyone would seem to think was the "right match" for him: A woman down on her luck in need of help.

Candy had three kids. She was married to an abusive man for about ten years before she finally got up the nerve to leave him. When Phil met Candy, she was only just one month removed from her divorce. Obviously, the whole ugly experience was still fresh on her mind, so Phil and Candy had something to commiserate over: Crazy exes and the awfulness of divorce.

Phil and Candy texted and spoke on the phone every single day for weeks. Sometimes multiple times per day. When

Phil didn't have his kids, he would go visit Candy… and vice versa. Their relationship started off VERY *"hot and heavy."* Lots of emotional and physical intimacy between the two of them. Phil felt like a kid in a candy store. Everything just seemed to click with Candy.

Then the texts from Candy became less frequent. She took longer to reply. Her answers were very short. This made Phil anxious. He could feel her pulling away. He asked Candy if everything was okay. At first, she would explain her quietness as just being stressed about work and kids. Then she cancelled on a weekend getaway they had planned. Then she went an entire day without replying to Phil's texts. That's when he knew that something was officially wrong. He angrily confronted her about her odd behavior, and she admitted that yes, she had lost feelings for him. She wasn't ready for this level of a relationship. She needed to back away.

Phil called up his friend to vent. His friend didn't seem that surprised. *"Dude… I'm sorry man, but did you see her Facebook page?"* Phil immediately flipped over to his Facebook app and saw the evidence. Candy was back with her abusive ex.

Phil was crushed. He found my site and booked a session with me right away. Phil said what a lot of men in his situation say: *"In a way, this feels worse than the divorce."* After seeing the worst that life can dish out, Phil felt like this connection with Candy was God's way of finally rewarding him. *"Sorry about that hell I just put you through,"* God said. *"Here's a beautiful young woman that will make you feel like a king again.*" Only to have the rug pulled out from under him. *"Psych! Just kidding. She's just like your ex-wife. Broken."*

I can sympathize with Phil. I've been down that same road, as have many other men learning about life after their failed marriages.

Phil wasn't ready to date. Candy wasn't ready, either. They were just two hurt individuals that were forced together by well-meaning friends. If Candy had her head on straight, she would've told Phil up front she was only one month out from her divorce, and not ready to date or do anything beyond a little chitchat. If Phil was also thinking clearly, he would have been polite, but would have slowly backed away from the freshly divorced gal with three kids and an abusive ex-husband. He would have known that it was just way too soon for both of them.

Lesson learned. Phil experienced the heart-wrenching torment that is the Rebound Chick.

CHAPTER 5
FOCUS ON YOU

KEEP BUSY

Just like when trying to break an addiction to a drug such as alcohol, getting over your ex is a really difficult thing to do. Your body and brain will say, *"Now, hold on a second. Wait… let's talk about this first."* Unfortunately, there is no magic bullet cure for getting over your ex in a hurry. You can't take medication to make all the pain go away and never return. Getting over a lost love is a gradual process you can either expedite or make drag on for YEARS. I have talked to men who have literally watched their exes have multiple affairs, divorce them, remarry, divorce again, remarry again… and yet the men STILL have feelings for their ex-wives and dream of getting back together. Why? Because they're still addicted. They are still taking the occasional shot of the ex-wife whiskey instead of putting the bottle down and stopping cold turkey. They're still hanging around the proverbial bar on Fridays. They didn't do the really hard but necessary work of breaking that bond. If they did, they would look at these women with the extreme disdain and eventual indifference that they deserve and not daydream about one day getting back together.

If there's one piece of advice I give to EVERY man trying to get over a failed relationship, it's to *"KEEP BUSY."* For the sake of your sanity, your overall health, and your future on this planet, you absolutely must have things to do. This is the work needed to move on in life and break the bond with your ex. You need goals to work towards. You need to accomplish things. No, you cannot just do your normal day-to-day routine of work, come home, collapse on the couch, drink beer, and fall asleep. You need to put down on paper what you want to accomplish, outline the steps to accomplish these goals, and check them off as you go. When complete, you move on to the next goal. You do this again, and again, and again. You accomplish things. Lots of things. That's called living.

A recent article on the website Psychology Today talked about a phenomenon that was coined by researchers at UCLA studying depression: *"Empty Man Syndrome."* To quote the article:

"On one of my first days there, I heard my colleagues whisper-ing about a patient. One mumbled something about 'empty' that I couldn't quite hear. I jumped into the conversation and asked what they were talking about. She replied, 'I said he has empty-man syndrome.' Intrigued, I asked her what that was. It was a term she came up with to describe certain men with depression. It applies to guys in their forties and up who are single or divorced, don't have any friends, are unemployed or stuck in a job they don't like and have no real hobbies. I asked why she came up with a term for this, and she sighed, 'Be-cause they don't ever seem to get better.'"

Men get depressed. It happens. Thanks to our innate need to provide for and protect our loved ones, we can easily allow the mundane nature of our work and parenting lives to get in the way of doing all the other things we need to do to keep our brains and bodies healthy. We all know the dad who works a ton of hours and comes home and collapses and does it all over again the next day. You may have even been that guy. If you don't exercise both your mind and your body in the way that is right for you, they will both atrophy. Being in a marriage and having kids tends to gradually accomplish this negative spiral for many men.

There are two important things that every man needs in order to avoid the slippery slope of chronic depression:

1. **Social Support.** As much as I say you don't NEED to have Real Love or marriage to be a complete man, you DO need to have some type of regular social contact and support network in place. You need family, friends, and loved ones that are there for you in times of need. You need consistent human contact in a meaningful way. Socialization is a basic human need. This is why solitary confinement is considered an inhumane form of punishment. It literally drives you crazy.

2. **Feeling like you have a purpose in life.** This one is especially true for men after their marriages dissolve. Men often use their marriages/kids/families as their sole purpose in life, so to suddenly yank that away is absolutely horrible and life-questioning. Many alcohol, drug and food problems start when men hit rock bottom after divorce. When you have no purpose in life, you will fill the void with something… and it's usually nothing good.

Being more social and finding a purpose (or multiple purposes) are not insurmountable tasks. Most of the time you can accomplish both via the action of going out and

DOING things. You need to take action. You need to build momentum. Take the first step, then another step, and so on. Once you get up and get going, it's amazing what you can accomplish. I know better than anyone that first step is the toughest. The good news is that the first step is simply using your brain and asking yourself, *"Okay... what is it I WANT?"*

For most men, they have an inkling of what it is they WANT to do, but it's a matter of actually putting together the plan, and incrementally taking the steps necessary to accomplish the goal. The good news is that accomplishing these goals also puts you in touch with a growing circle of new friends and loved ones that help you along the way. It's a win-win situation. It's just a matter of kicking yourself in the butt and getting started.

CHOOSING YOUR MISSION

Get out a pen and paper. It's time to write a list. I want you to throw aside all of your preconceptions about what you have the time to do. Pretend you have all the time and energy in the world. Get yourself in a child-like mindset of adventure and possibilities. Don't worry about anyone judging you. Your nag of an ex-wife isn't here. Your mom and dad don't need to know about this. Keep it to yourself.

Now, write on a list the things you like and want to do. Could be things you already do from time to time, or it could be things you always wanted to do. Here's an example of a list you could write. Just play pretend and go along with it for now.

1. Joining a gym.
2. Gardening.
3. Remodeling the house.
4. Rebuilding old cars.
5. Learning to fly a drone and take aerial photos.
6. Skiing.
7. Scuba diving.
8. Ballroom dancing.
9. Getting a pilot's license.
10. Learning archery.

Those are just ten things that came off the top of my head.
It's a collection of the different things I have heard men and
friends say over the years. Some of these items may seem
a little more *out there* or more unobtainable than others.
Maybe you're like many divorced men and time and money
are both difficult to come by right now and that affects your
short-term goals. That's totally understandable.

Look at your list and put a star next to those items that can
be started right away. You need some quick wins under your
belt. We don't want to get bogged down in details of the
goals that aren't realistic until five years from now. The big
dream stuff is great, and they are on your list for a reason,
but we can't tackle them right now. For me personally, I
would say learning to fly a plane would NOT be a realistic
goal for me in my life. I have too many other things going
on and getting my pilot's license takes many hours and lots
of money that I simply don't have. Scuba diving? Not going

to happen anytime soon. There is an indoor scuba school about an hour from here that I could go to and take classes, but that's not high on my list of must-do things. Scuba diving is a skill I may use once or twice from now until the day I die. Maybe one day I'll look into it, but not right now. Not a big deal. Instead, for me, I would put a star next to going to the gym, gardening, and ballroom dancing.

Now that you have put a star next to those realistic and attainable goals, it's time to put a plan of action into place. First, prioritize what you have starred on the list. If three of your items are starred, look at those and rank them according to what lights your fire. Which one really makes you say, *"Yeah… I could do that. That would be really fun and interesting."* That is your number one priority right now. We are tackling just one thing at a time. Again… we're after quick wins.

You now need to put together a set of steps needed to get started and to maintain the hobby/goal/activity. For example, if I really wanted to learn ballroom dancing (I know… just go with it), the steps would be:

1. Research classes. Pick a school.
2. Set time to go take a lesson.
3. Attend the lesson.
4. Go every single week for the next three months, no matter what.

What's going to happen after you climb off the couch and attend classes during those three months? You will meet new people. Probably a lot of women. Women are more social creatures, so they are usually the first ones to sign up for any new group activities or classes. You will probably be one of the few men in the class. You will meet an all-around different group of adventurous adults who all had the same idea you had: *"It might be kinda cool to learn how to dance properly like I've seen on TV."* They're all in the same boat. They're in the class to better themselves and enjoy life. When you surround yourself with such positive and outgoing people, your perspective on life changes. You become more energized. Momentum builds. Somebody in the class that you became friends with suggests that you should also try out a yoga class with them. They've been going for a few weeks and it's amazing. Their back has never felt better. Oh, and the chicks in their yoga class make the ballroom dancers look like a nursing home!

Next thing you know, you're now in a yoga class once a week, staring at young, in-shape women sweating in tights. You suddenly love yoga. Now you regularly attend both a dance and a yoga class that you weren't taking before. After a few weeks, you decide to give yoga a three month try as well. You enjoy ballroom dancing so much that you're going to keep it going past the three-month period, at least until the teacher says you're good enough to leave or maybe graduate to a different class. With those two classes going on every week, you'll notice the pounds start to melt off. Your agility and cardio capacity go way up. Flexibility is way up. You're just all around healthier and more vibrant. You enjoy the classes so much that you don't groan and belly ache over having to go. You sometimes even throw in an extra class here and there if time allows. Positive momentum is building. You try to recruit friends and family to join you.

Now that you've added those two activities to your regular weekly schedule, they don't feel like extra work. They just simply replaced the pointless TV time or the time you spent playing Xbox and watching porn. Now you think about the NEXT step. You want to add something else to the mix. The positive snowball is building. Once you get going and you get some *"wins"* under your belt, it's hard to stop the progress. It just happens. Then the end of the year comes, and you look back and say, *"Damn. I got a lot of shit done."*

TAKE CONTROL

Whatever your mission may be, there needs to be an overall theme of *"taking control"* of your life. You need to throw out all the "woe is me" notions of life doing things to you. Hey, life always presents you with very real obstacles and very real opportunities. That's just what life does. You can make all the plans you want, but life may decide it has something else entirely in store for you. *"Man plans and God laughs."* Sometimes it seems like the stupid obstacles way outnumber any positive opportunities you may have in the foreseeable future. It sometimes may even seem overwhelmingly negative, to the point of being one big cosmic joke. The car breaks down, the dishwasher leaks all over the kitchen, you stepped in dog shit on your way to work, your boss announces that you're getting laid off, and your wife suddenly wants a divorce. Hey, it happens. So, how do you respond? Do you look at the cards you are dealt and figure out how to play them, or do you throw your cards down on the table and pout about what a shitty hand you have? Which option do you think will generate actual results and a way out of the shitstorm of problems?

It amazes me how many men go on and on about their life situations, as if they are telling me about a novel they are reading. They talk about themselves almost in the third person. They're detached. Out of control. Helpless. Sometimes they are frozen by indecisiveness. Sometimes they KNOW exactly what they need to do next, but it's just too damn hard and they are too damn tired. They have zero momentum. They need some help.

You need to take a moment and *"look down"* on yourself from above. If you're a religious person, maybe it helps to put yourself in God's shoes for a moment. If you're a science fiction guy, maybe look at you and your life as one big computer simulation. You're in a giant video game of life. When you are presented with all this overwhelmingly negative bullshit in life, it's like meeting the video game *"boss"* at the end of the level. Do you throw down the controller and say *"fuck it"* because beating the boss is impossible? Do you start all over at the beginning and get to the boss again and try out a different strategy? Maybe you should go on the internet and look for a cheat code that will give you unlimited firepower so you can breeze through the boss and make it to the next level. Whatever the solution is, there IS a solution there. Sometimes it's just a matter of picking up the damn controller and getting to work. Make the little guy (you) jump over the fire, climb up on the moving platform, grab the golden key, beat the dragon, and save the princess.

You gotta take control. Today. Move forward. DO SOME-THING. Get help if you need it. Your future self will thank you.

TAKE CARE OF YOUR BODY

Okay, let's set aside the imaginary world of ballroom dancing and yoga for now. I used those two examples because they illustrate how you can really step outside of your comfort zone, leave the house, attend some classes, use your body in new ways, and mingle with a new and successful group of people. For many of you, going to a class like that just ain't gonna happen. You could be working two jobs and have three kids to watch full time. You could live out in the middle of nowhere and Walmart is the only sign of civilization within fifty miles of you. Maybe the closest thing to yoga in your area is watching the town drunks collapse in awkward positions at the public park. Hey, I grew up in the middle of nowhere America. Trust me, I get it.

Let's think about what you CAN do right now. Remember, your final to-do list should be realistic and attainable. You need some wins under your belt. You need to build up some real and serious momentum. There is one subject that should always be at or near the top of your mission list. It's the one thing that you have absolutely ZERO excuse to ignore. It's the one thing you walk around with every single day, 24/7. It's the one thing you probably have ignored far too much over the years. We're talking about your body. Simply put, you need to get your ass in shape and take care of yourself. Your body should be your #1 mission in life. The good news is that building up your body and improving your health will probably be the most rewarding mission you've ever been on.

All missions are deemed worthwhile and sustainable when you achieve something along the way. If you decided you wanted to write a book (like I'm doing right now), you get started typing away at your computer, maybe not even caring about the outline or organization of the book. Along the way, you check the total word count, stop and read sections out loud… and you smile. *I'm actually doing this. I'm going to be an author when it's all said and done. How cool is that?"* As you progress, the organization of the book takes shape. Chapters begin to form. Paragraphs are moved around. Sections are deleted. Thoughts come to you out of thin air. *"Serendipity,"* they call it. You're in a state of flow. Hours fly by like minutes.

When you decide to take on your body as a mission, you see results pretty quickly. Eating right and exercising just makes you feel and look a lot better. The pants are looser. The shirts fit better. The blood pressure goes down. You're able to walk up twenty flights of stairs with no problem. You can lift your kids like they're nothing. Each little moment is a step towards building momentum. Next thing you know, you're at the Mexican restaurant telling your kids to keep the basket of chips the hell away from you and you're ordering the grilled chicken dinner. You can't wait to hit the next physical milestone, and a dumb basket of salty tortilla chips will not stop you from getting there. You are a man on a mission.

SLEEP

I put this first for a reason. Men, most of you are chronically sleep-deprived. You are not getting the amount of sleep that you need to be at your best level, both physically and mentally. It's time that we set aside our antiquated notions of staying up late at night, watching TV with a beer in hand and getting up at the crack of dawn to tackle our workday. Getting up early is fine, as long as you get to bed early, too. Don't think that working on less than eight hours of sleep per day somehow makes you a more productive man. In fact, it does just the opposite.

You need sleep to rebuild both your brain and your body. Think of sleep as the time your body says, *"Okay, we have some much-needed cleaning and repairs to do, and we need you to pass out while we do it."* If you're routinely cutting back on your sleep, below the scientifically proven threshold of eight hours, you're interrupting that important cleaning and rebuilding process. Some important tasks will be left undone. When you wake up too early, little janitors and repairmen running around in your body throw their tools down in disgust.

"Well, I guess once again I'm not mopping the bathroom floor! This is going to get really gross in a hurry if I don't get to do my job!"

We know for a fact that lack of adequate sleep puts you at risk for:

- Heart disease.
- High blood pressure.
- Diabetes.
- Lower sex drive.
- Depression.
- Weight gain.
- Advanced aging.
- Memory loss.
- Increased risk of Alzheimer's.

If you routinely sleep less than six to seven hours per night, you increase your risk of cancer by 50%.

Getting sleep is no joke. The days of bragging about getting by on five hours of shut eye are long gone. Thanks to science, we now know what a horrible idea that is. Feeling groggy at 2:00pm every day? Get a quick nap in. Do whatever you can to shut your eyes for twenty minutes. Sneak away from your office if you have to. Your body needs that rebuilding time. You will be a more productive human if you listen to your body and get the rest it NEEDS to function properly.

Get your butt to bed early. Your life depends on it.

YOU ARE WHAT YOU EAT

Contrary to what many people may think, if you really want to make yourself look and feel better, a good 90% of the work revolves around your diet. As fitness gurus will tell you: *"Abs start in the kitchen."* You can work your tail off in the gym, bench press the equivalent of a small elephant, sweat so much you could fill a baby pool, and you can quickly erase ALL of that hard work with a diet of pizza, chips, and beer. The muscle you worked so hard to build will be hidden under a thick layer of blubber. The guy who works 1/4 as much as you do in the gym but eats a healthy diet will look better and be a lot healthier than your fat-but-strong self.

I can't tell you how many guys I see at the gym that bust their butts on a regular basis and have absolutely nothing to show for it. For YEARS they look the same. Sure, their bench press and dead lift gradually go up (something they will undoubtedly tell everyone within earshot), but as far as people outside of the gym and their own doctors are concerned, they're the woefully out-of-shape fat guys who are one pizza slice away from a stroke. They could do a complete one eighty change if they simply stopped shoving crap into their pieholes. The strong guy at the gym that looks like a sumo wrestler is probably just six to twelve months of healthy eating away from turning heads and looking like a legit *"holy shit"* lean muscular guy that everyone admires.

To keep it brief, stop putting unhealthy shit into your body. Don't complicate this. Don't play dumb. You KNOW what the *"unhealthy shit"* is. It's not rocket science. Stop bullshitting yourself and everyone around you.

It's easy to SAY, but it's not necessarily easy to DO. The lure of unhealthy food is incredibly strong. That crap is literally engineered to appeal to your mouth and your brain and cause you to eat more and more and more. The snack companies have this stuff down to a science. Everything from the proper amount of sweet and saltiness to the mouthfeel and crunch. It's been tested again and again until they get it just right. Then they put it on the market and rake in the millions as the world gets more obese, and type 2 diabetes and heart disease kill us by the thousands. They're drug pushers and we're all their loyal junkies.

Hey, don't get me wrong, I love snacks. They're freaking amazing. Salty crunchy crap is my heroin. Put a giant bowl of Chex Mix in front of me, and that bastard is decimated in minutes. That's why I can't have it in the house. I don't buy chips. No pretzels. No crackers. No deliciously perfect Chex Mix. If they were here, they would be gone in no time That's my personal boundary I have to put up to keep my health in check. I get fat easily. I'm not some flawless fitness Adonis here. I'm a fat guy in an in-shape guy's body. It takes a lot of work for me to stay in shape. Is it worth it? Hell yeah. What's the alternative? It's not a pretty sight. Trust me.

Think about a horribly out-of-shape fifty-year-old fat dude with oxygen tubes in his nose sitting in a doctor's office listening to a concerned MD tell him about the dangers of congestive heart failure and how he needs to go on eight different medications and probably get his stomach stapled or else he's going to die. Think that guy is sitting there saying, *"Yeah, but doc… those pizzas and beer were fucking awesome"*? No. The poor slob is thinking, *"What have I done? I don't want to die like this. Jesus Christ, what a waste of a life."* If you're a young guy, take it from older guys like me… fifty will be here TOMORROW. The years just fly by. You don't want to waste those precious years because something tasted great and made you feel happy for five minutes. You're not some bored housewife crying while shoving ice cream in your face and chasing it down with a bottle of wine. You're a man. Act like one. Put the cupcakes down.

I'm telling you, if you simply start eating like a guy who cares about his health… you're going to feel and look a thousand times better. If you combine healthy eating with a regular, rigorous exercise program, the sky is the limit on just how good you can look and feel. A whole new world will open up to you.

WHAT DIET IS RIGHT FOR YOU?

The problem for a lot of guys that decide to get in shape is that the fitness world is so damn confusing. There are literally hundreds of diet and fitness plans out there. There are vegetarian diets, all meat diets, ketogenic diets, high carb diets… you name it, and somebody has *"proof"* that their way of eating is the absolute best possible way, period. My opinion? Well, I just go by what the science tells us, and it's pretty simple:

The only successful diet is one that YOU can maintain consistently over a long period of time.

That's it. If that means a ketogenic diet of meats and greens and very low to no carbs works best for you AND you actually enjoy it with no major urges for carbs and no cheating… congrats, you found your meal plan for life (yes, for life). Maybe you find that a *"Mediterranean diet"* is more up your alley. Maybe you have personal reasons to go vegetarian. Maybe you learn you need a cheat meal just once a week to keep you sane and active. Maybe you eat a very strict diet during the week and work out like an animal so you can get away with an entire cheat day of sweets and pizza every Saturday, and your waistline stays small, and your health doesn't suffer (lucky you).

Every person is different. If you're on a meal plan that has you regularly crashing and bingeing on junk food, gaining five pounds, and then starting over again to try to lose those five pounds… and then do it over again… only to end up gaining twelve pounds after twelve months, well then you are not on the right meal plan for you. That will not work out for you long-term. You're setting yourself up for catastrophic failure and a myriad of health problems. Time for Plan B. What is Plan B? No idea. I'm not you. That's up to you to test out and see what works best for you and your body and lifestyle. But first, you need to do the work of determining what your current starting point is and go from there.

GET THEE TO A DOCTOR

Prior to any kind of diet change, I highly recommend you go to the doc and get a full workup done. Check out your blood lipids, your thyroid, and your hormone levels. If your thyroid levels are out of whack and your testosterone is at the level of a ninety-year-old man (more common than you may think), you may need to take medications that will get you to a baseline *"normal"* level before starting on your healthy journey. You can do a super strict healthy diet and work your ass off in the gym five days a week, but if your total testosterone is one hundred twenty (when it should be closer to eight hundred), then you are just going to be beating your head against the wall in frustration. You'll follow a plan for months and just end up looking like dog shit. Then you'll switch plans. Then the new plan won't work, either. Then you'll give up. You'll go back to eating crap and skipping the gym, and you'll be worse off than you were before. If you're going to do something, do it right. Go get checked out by your doc as soon as possible.

At the time of this writing, there is a bit of a medical/fitness renaissance going on as it pertains to unique individual preventative care and fitness. What we're learning goes beyond simply saying, *"everyone is different."* Thanks to relatively inexpensive at-home DNA testing companies like 23andMe. com, you can spit into a vial, send it in the mail, and a short time later get a detailed report telling you everything about yourself from your ancestry to your predisposition to specific diseases and disorders. It's absolutely ground-breaking for personal health and fitness. The concept of *"guesswork"* and a *"one system is best for everyone"* is going right out the window.

I used a combination of 23andMe.com and DNAfit.com to learn that I have genes that suggest I am very carb intolerant, a slow metabolizer of caffeine, intolerant of booze/ marijuana, and I'm especially sensitive to salt. I don't need as much vitamin D as I thought I did. I need to watch eating too much charred/smoked meats, and I need to eat more cruciferous veggies. I also need to up my intake of vitamins A, C, and B12. Workout-wise, I am more inclined to do best at endurance sports (a shock to me… a longtime weight trainer) and I have the capacity for a high VO2 max (the amount of oxygen I can use during intense exercise). I also have a higher likelihood of injury from working out.

As the science gets better, information about my specific DNA profile will continue to trickle in. On a regular basis, I get reports showing my likelihood of type 2 diabetes, dementia, macular degeneration, etc. I find it all to be extremely interesting and can't wait to see what advancements in the DNA world take place over the next ten years. Soon, we will be able to tailor our diets and fitness regimens to fit our specific individual needs and limitations. No longer will we ask our in-shape buddy, *"So, what kind of workout should I do? How about diet?"* You'll know exactly what YOU need to do to look good and live long and healthy. It may be a completely different prescription compared to your buddy.

TESTOSTERONE REPLACEMENT THERAPY

If you've read my website, you know I am on Testosterone Replacement Therapy (TRT). I inject an oil-based compounded testosterone solution into my butt twice a week, every week. I've been on this regimen for over eight years now. It works well for me. It takes me to a physical and mental state that I otherwise would not be in. Does that make me less of a man? Maybe. With every shot I take, I'm admitting that I am not a natural badass. I'm a guy who found out he had a deficiency, took meds, and felt better. It's no different from a person who takes any other medication to bring them to a baseline level of health.

There is a strange stigma around TRT. There's an obvious level of scrutiny and shaming that you don't see with other *"wellness"* therapies. Why? Because we're talking about treating men. If I was a woman going to the doctor and saying, *"I would like to stop my periods because they are heavy and very painful,"* or just simply, *"I would like to go on some form of birth control so that I can have sex worry free,"* the doctor would give me a literal menu of choices to choose from, and all will drastically alter my hormonal makeup. I could take a shot every few months, pills every day, implants, etc. Are there dangers to these drugs? Of course. Some dangers can be pretty significant. So then, why are doctors so eager and willing to prescribe these drugs? Simply put, the freedom to manipulate your body as you see fit and to take control of your own fertility is an empowering statement of female freedom in an otherwise oppressive society. The woman finally gets to control what goes on with her body. With every pill she swallows, she is saying, *"I'M in charge of ME."*

It cannot be overstated: The birth control pill transformed the sexual landscape in the western world, and the medical industry hasn't looked back since. If you're a doctor and a female patient comes to you wanting to go on birth control, you don't question her motivations. You would never in a million years say, *"Why? You're supposed to be making babies, young lady. You're a woman. That's what you do. Pills aren't really natural, anyway. They can be dangerous. Have you tried condoms? If you must do birth control, that's the way to go."* If you said that, you'd be out of a job faster than you can say #metoo.

Now, pretend for a moment that you go to the doctor and ask for a blood test so that you can see where your testosterone levels are. First thing the doc says: *"Why?"* You explain that you're getting older, and you have certain symptoms that are concerning you. You list the symptoms and show the doc the data that shows that these symptoms could be alleviated by reaching proper levels of testosterone. You just want to see where your levels are at right now. The doctor chuckles. *"These are all perfectly natural things you're experiencing. Welcome to getting older. If you find you are depressed, I can certainly put you on an SSRI. There are also some great therapists in the area you can talk to."* If you push further on the matter, the doc may get hostile. You're not only questioning his authority, but you're now officially one of THOSE guys. You will hear how not everyone is a He-Man, and you just need to accept your lot in life. Plus, there are numerous dangers around testosterone therapy. They will tell you about prostate cancer, heart attacks, strokes, etc. Then he will pat you on the back and chuckle as he motions you out of his office. *"Let me know if you want to try out Prozac. I have many patients on it with wonderful results."*

Many doctors throw mind-altering (and arguably dangerous) substances like SSRIs, and even opioids, at their patients like they are parade candy, but ask about testosterone… and watch your doctor's mood abruptly change.

You immediately go from being a regular boring patient to some dumb guy having a midlife crisis. Why is that, exactly? Why is it that even a guy who has done a ton of homework, brings literature to his doctor, and asks for a simple blood test, is laughed at and dismissed so quickly? I think it's primarily a sexist attitude. *"Not everyone is a He-Man,"* your doc may bluntly say. It's a not-so-nice way of saying, *"Know your place in society. Go tend to your kids, change diapers, and sit at a desk all day. The manly stuff is best left to the real men who don't need a shot in the butt."* In short, when it comes to men, nobody likes an imposter. Society wants the real thing. We want a natural. The second that somebody picks up on you TRYING to be more *"manly"* (being fake) they will turn on you. The very people you trust with your health will blatantly laugh at you. Your friends and family may also join in on the fun. Not unexpectedly, these are also the same people that will dissuade you from all forms of self-improvement. They like you in the comfortable, boring Provider role that you are in. If you suddenly want to switch things up and change your role, they will pull every trick in the book to keep you where you are. More often than not, the first thing they go to is using shame to manipulate you.

I'm not going to tell you that TRT is right for you. I'm no doctor. All I can tell you is my own personal experience:

- I gained muscle.
- I lost body fat.
- I lowered my anxiety/stress.
- I feel more confident.

Have there been negative side effects? Yes. For one, I have learned that I need to control my estrogen levels via an additional medication called Arimidex. To oversimplify the science behind it, your body may try to counteract the higher testosterone levels you are introducing by increasing the opposing hormone known as estrogen. This is done by the aromatase enzyme, via a process in the body called aromatization. To counteract this, you can take an aromatase inhibitor (AI) like Arimidex (there are other types and brands of AI medications). Not everyone on TRT needs an AI, but I did. Without it, I would bloat and grow breasts. Seriously. But, if I take too much AI, it will lower my estrogen to levels that are way too low and I will experience joint pain, emotional flatness, lowered libido, and an increase chance of heart disease. Luckily, I have learned how to avoid this with proper minimal dosing.

Overall, my experience with TRT has been positive. Since I've been on it, my blood pressure has not gone up, my cholesterol levels are fine, and my hormonal levels are within balance. One thing that crept up was my red blood cell count. To alleviate that, I make sure I drink a lot of water and I donate blood. Problem solved.

Two more negatives to consider when on testosterone:

1. **You are on it for life.** This isn't a "one shot and you're cured" kind of deal. This is a regular routine of taking your shot (or applying your cream) every single week for the rest of your life. Oh, sure, you can stop your TRT at any time, but your body will go back down to testosterone levels low-

er than they were before, and it may take additional drugs to help restart your body's natural production again (HCG, for example). You'll eventually be back at your low baseline level and feel like crap all over again. Many men don't last long at this stage. Once you have felt *"normal"* or better, you don't want to go back.

2. Fertility will most likely be lowered or gone completely. Trying to have a kid? Plan to have any in the near future? Do yourself a favor and go get some of your sperm frozen and stored. Go to the fertility clinic, run a few batches, and put that baby batter on ice. It will cost a small fortune, but you'll have to do it if you want to have kids in the future AND be on testosterone. Why? The little secret that nobody likes to tell you is that testosterone is a potent form of birth control for many men. By introducing an external source of testosterone to the body, your testes will shut down their own production and, subsequently, the production of sperm. It's your body's way of saying, *"I see I'm getting my testosterone from an outside source now. Welp, no need for these testicles anymore."* Yes, your balls may atrophy and shrink down in size. This can be alleviated by taking a compound known as HCG (another shot). Even while on HCG and sporting a full set of testicles, many men report their sperm count as at or near zero. In short, if you want to get a woman pregnant, you probably need to be off of testosterone or have some potent sperm ready to thaw out.

WORKING OUT

Ninety percent of how you look and feel may be determined

by your diet and sleep, but the remaining 10% is built by working out. Training. Sweating. Hitting the gym. Busting your ass. Doing it repeatedly. Pushing yourself. Going for a walk is fine and dandy (and very good for you), but it's not working out. It's not busting your ass. That's what old sedentary people do after their doc puts them on blood pressure meds and recommends they move instead of sitting all day long. *"Working out"* goes beyond that. We're talking about training yourself. It means shocking your body so that it is forced to build muscle and lose body fat. It's going to mean stepping outside of your comfort zone in a big way. It's also a shit ton of fun and changes your life in so many ways.

For you guys with limited funds and time, the good news is that the gym is not needed to gain that extra 10%. It's great to have access to a large number of weights and machines to sculpt your physique, but you can attain a fantastic level of fitness by doing bodyweight exercises in your bedroom. Push-ups, burpees, dips, yoga, squats, lunges, jumping… these are ready to do right this minute. You just need a floor and your body. That's it. Want to kick it up a notch? Go online and order a jump rope, a kettlebell or two, some bands, and a medicine ball. Now you have another twelve months' worth of exercises you can do before you get bored and need something more advanced.

I could go on and on about an exact workout routine, but I won't bother. There are so many out there. Just like diet, you need one that is right for you… and one that you will maintain consistently over a long period (with positive results). My recommendation is to mix things up. Do various things to keep it interesting and keep the body guessing: Military-style calisthenics, bodybuilding style weight training, steady state cardio, high-intensity interval training, power-lifting, martial arts, gymnastics, yoga… the list goes on and on. Pick what you like. Do it. Then do it again. Consistently. Have fun with it. If it gets stale, try something else out.

Yes, you can overdo it. *"Overtraining"* is real, especially for you older guys out there. You want to look forward to going to the gym or doing your home workout. You want to approach this mission with energy and joy. You don't want to feel so sore that you need three days of rest to recover. You don't want to break your body down and get a sore throat and cold chills the day after your workout. That's your immune system telling you to cut it out and back off. You want to sleep, eat, and drink enough to provide the fuel you need to hit your workouts with motivation and positive energy.

For my personality type, I tend to REALLY get into a new hobby/interest and go as hard as I can, get burned out, and move on to something else. Working out is no different. If I walk into the gym, I want to see how much weight I can lift and try to squeeeeeze out that last repetition until I reach the point of absolute failure. Then I move on to the next exercise and do it again. Three sets… gradually increasing the weight… absolute failure. Then on to the next exercise. That plan worked when I was younger. I put on some good muscle that way when I was in my twenties. Now, that would be a quick way to injury and certain burnout. Now I need to tell myself to hold back a little. I usually finish a workout set well short of my absolute failure. Now when I do an exercise, I concentrate on feeling the muscles work. I focus on my form and proper range of motion. I finish my sets with some gas left in the tank. I take a breather, gather myself, get a drink of water, and then continue on with my workout. My workouts are usually around an hour to an hour and a half long and do I feel drained… but in a good way. I don't feel like I've been hit by a truck. My muscles feel full, my head feels clearer, my clothes are drenched, and I'm ready to tackle the rest of my day. That's the state of Zen you want to be in as a result of working out.

Again, I'm not going to tell YOU what to do to build YOUR body. Use Google to come up with different workout ideas. YouTube has an endless number of videos. AthleanX is a great program if you want to spend some money. Maybe find a good trainer to help you out. Maybe go to one of the many garage-style gyms that are popping up all over the place. They usually have a prescribed plan in place and a series of stations set up for people to do. You go around and complete each station at your own pace (with the guidance of a coach). It's usually a good combination of cardio, high-intensity interval training, and lifting weights. My wife goes to such a gym (along with two different yoga classes). She loves it, and she's not a natural gym-goer by any means. She likes that she is told what to do, she does it, she gets better each time, and her body thanks her for it. That's what you want to do. Find a program that helps you achieve the little, important wins along the way. Like with anything in life, momentum is key. You need to move forward in a positive direction on a regular basis. The result will be a completely new you looking back at yourself in the mirror.

Do it. Your life will change immensely. Personal health and fitness is one of the building blocks of a foundation for a good life. Once you have that sturdy foundation, everything else just seems to click into place.

TRYING TO LOSE FAT? BE PATIENT

Losing body fat is a tricky thing. For those that are morbidly obese, they see the biggest results within the shortest time frame. Take a five-hundred-pound guy and put him on a healthy diet and exercise program, and he could easily lose ten pounds per week. After all, it takes a lot of work for a five-hundred-pound guy to maintain that huge unhealthy shape. It takes lots and lots of eating high-calorie foods over a long period. It's not an easy job. Take away the excess food, and get him moving in new ways, and his body sighs in relief and starts melting away the fat cells. *"Finally, I can stop being so damn fat. That really sucked."*

Take a muscular two-hundred-pound guy at sixteen per-cent bodyfat who works out regularly, but he would really like to be one hundred eighty-five pounds at eight percent bodyfat. That is a whole different story. His body wants to maintain those two hundred pounds and will do all it can to stay there. If you're in that boat, BE PATIENT. A half pound or a pound a week of weight loss is not bad at all. Keep it up and you'll see results, but it will be extremely tough. You will have to work A LOT harder and a lot smarter to get to that *"unnatural"* level of lean muscularity. As Lyle McDon-ald outlines in his book The Stubborn Fat Solution, the fat loss can sometimes seem to happen in *"whooshes."* You'll be eating at a deficit, working hard in the gym, and yet you notice the numbers on the scale go up two pounds. It makes no sense! Why bother working so hard? Then a few short days later, you'll notice you've lost four pounds. You gained two, but then you lost four, a net loss of two pounds. Why did this happen? Well, it may very well be your body increasing water retention in an effort to maintain weight, and then finally giving up and letting go of the water and some of those stubborn fat cells. I've noticed this phenomenon in my body. I'm not a gradual fat loser. My weight loss stalls, and then the fat and water whooshes off in bursts.

Want to look like those fitness models you see in the ads? Be aware of what you're getting yourself into. The use of anabolic steroids and other chemicals for burning fat and maintaining muscle is extremely common in the world of modeling. Those abs and veins you see online and in the magazines aren't *"natural."* That is an extreme state for the body to be in, and typically, they're in that shape for only a very short amount of time. Yes, the models are naturally gifted athletic people who look a lot better than most of us, but that extreme level of muscularity and low bodyfat that you see in the ads for supplements and exercise equipment is not an easy and normal state for them to maintain. Those people use whatever edge they can to achieve that *"whoa"* effect for the day of the photoshoot, and then they go back to their normal non-depleted states. Don't fall into the trap of comparing yourself to others, especially when the game is not a level playing field and what you're seeing is not at all realistic. You just work on being the best YOU possible.

Be realistic about your goals. Put your health first. Work hard, eat right, stay positive… and you'll be rewarded when you look in the mirror.

TAKE CARE OF YOUR MIND

This experience of divorce that you are going through is very tough. It is traumatic. No matter how tough of a guy you think you may be, you're going to need some help. If left to your own devices, you have a high chance of slipping into a very real and debilitating chronic depression. Once you string together several weeks of consistently ignoring your mental health needs, that sets into motion a cascading series of events that will shut you down mentally. That's not a good place to be, and one that is very tough to crawl out of.

There is absolutely, positively nothing wrong with a man raising his hand and asking for help. Nothing. I know it seems that the world is out to get you, and nobody seems to give a shit, but we do. Often, your friends and loved ones feel weird about asking if you need help. If you're like a lot of guys, you have probably presented a *"tough guy"* front for years. You may not have been the most "emotionally open" guy in the world. Probably, you've unknowingly put up a lot of walls around you. The thought of them going up to you and extending a helping hand may seem to be really off-limits to them. It's going to take you setting aside your ego for a bit and saying, *"Help."* You'll may be surprised at who jumps to your aid.

Therapy is always a good idea. Sit down and talk to somebody, a professional, who has seen lots of people in your exact shoes and knows the proper course of action to get you over the hump. I realize that a lot of my readers live out in the middle of nowhere and finding a therapist on your schedule is maybe difficult, but there are options out there for you. We have partnered with a company called Better Help. They provide a virtual system for connecting with a real, qualified professional. They have a mobile app you can use to chat with them via text, email, video chat, audio phonically… it's a great way to work around your schedule. Go to betterhelp.com/dso and you get 10% off of your first month of service.

Our team at Help For Men is also there to help. We are NOT licensed mental health professionals of any kind, but we are a team of coaches that have been through what you have. We have guys who have endured divorce, military guys with experience with PTSD, guys who have turned their marriages around, guys who have a lot of luck in dating, and guys who have transformed themselves physically in huge ways. You can learn more at helpformen.com/coaching. On a side note, members of our HFM Brotherhood (helpformen.com/join) get to join our coaches in live meetings and also get big discounts on one-on-one coaching. Give it a shot for a month or two to see if you like it.

Whatever avenue you take is going to require that you reach out to others for help. You can't do this alone. I mean, technically, you COULD just stay inside your house all day and talk to nobody and wait for the pain to pass… but that's not a good idea. That's just a great way to expedite your journey to the wonderful world of depression. You're better than that and deserve to live a life communing with others. You have loved ones in your life. Sometimes you just have to go out and find them.

HANG OUT WITH MEN

I can't overstate this enough: You need to spend more time with other men. I know it's difficult. I can totally relate. While I have hundreds of guys I chat with in the HFM Brotherhood (our private men's group at helpformen.com), in real-life, I only have a handful of men I can call on. Most of them are too busy to do anything outside of the family home. If I see them, it's usually at a game or some other school function.

That's not a good thing.

Men need a tribe. A squad. We need a masculine group of people that we can fall back on. We need men that can relate to our frame of mind and our life struggles. Every single time that I have that rare moment of hanging out with guys, I always leave saying the same thing: *"Man, I need to do that more often."* I experience a very real high after sitting down and talking about life with other men. It's like I, as a man, am naturally wired to spend time with guys and away from the woman and kids. My brain rewards me by making me feel better. It's saying, *"Yes! Do more of that! Go hang out with dudes!"* As I have learned in my post-divorce life, that's easier said than done.

Why men? Can't you get a sense of belonging and the social connection when hanging out with women? If you find yourself at a school function and you're surrounded by moms, isn't it a good thing to get friendly and have meaningful conversations with them? Yes, of course! But, it's not the same as hanging out with men. Nowhere near the same.

Men bring a completely different energy to the table. Some may perceive this energy from men as being *"challenging"* or even *"intimidating."* Some may feel that their connections with women seem to be more intimate and more genuine than their interactions with men. Usually, men that favor women over men for their socializing have a form of social anxiety. They feel nervous and threatened around other men, and yet they feel special and *"nice"* around women.

There's a natural hierarchy at play when interacting with men, and nobody wants to feel like the guy low on the totem pole. If you're a physically small guy, a shy guy, or a guy who is unsuccessful financially, it may be very tough for you to introduce yourself to a new group of men. You may feel like they judge you. They instantly size you up. They poke and prod to determine your worth. All of that is, in fact, completely true. You know what else is true? This same thing happens with the ladies you meet, too.

Every socially anxious guy who favors the ladies' group says the same thing: They like being the nice, social, sweet, funny guy amongst the group of women. It makes them feel special. They're different. In their own way, they are at the top of that social totem pole. They're a unique male creature in this little zoo of gossiping females. This gets him positive attention. Or so he thinks. What many men in this position, young and old, eventually recognize is that they are not so special after all. They are seen, in fact, as one of the ladies. For most men in their position, that's a bit disturbing. He may say or do something that tiptoes towards male hetero-sexuality, and the female group instantly turns on him. In a roundabout way, their sudden shift in attitude says, *"You're in this group as one of the girls. Not as a guy. That was the unspoken agreement we had. Bring that guy stuff in here, and you can get the hell out."*

As Dr. Robert Glover likes to say, you are the *"girlfriend with a penis."*

No love-starved heterosexual man wants to be in that role. It leads to a lot of heartache.

Guys in that situation KNOW they would gladly have sex with most, if not all, of the women in their friend group. The ladies know that, too. It's just an unspoken understand-ing. The man wants sex, and the girls don't look at him in that way. He hangs around hoping that maybe one day they will change their minds. The women never intend to change their minds, but they will gladly enjoy the favors of this *"friendship."* I say *"friendship"* in quotes because, can it ever really be a genuine friendship? Sure, you can be friendly… but TRUE friendship? Deep platonic love and respect for each other? No. It can't happen. Human behavior dictates that the underlying theme of sexuality will always color your thoughts and actions. That doesn't bode well for form-ing a strong bond based on friendship. It's just a friendly facade.

With men, no such facade exists. The softness and nuance that comes with female communication is gone. Everything

is blunt. Everything is out in the open, warts and all. Sometimes that is a little gross and off-putting, but often, with
time and the right group, it can be a breeding ground for
extremely close and vulnerable relationships. I have spoken
to many men who have made a concerted effort to reach
out to form friendships with other men. They usually report
back that it took a bit to break the ice, but once they did,
they realized just how crucial that bond can be. They were
pleasantly surprised at just how nice and open these new
male friends were. It made their female friend group seem
simple and shallow in comparison. In defense of the ladies,
they can probably never feel safe enough to be truly open
when in the presence of a man… no matter how much of a
"fellow girlfriend" he may be.

OBSTACLES

Other than the obvious hard work, dedication and discipline needed to complete your goals and missions in life, there are more not-so-obvious obstacles in the way of you becoming the man you're truly capable of being. You thought this was going to be easy?

The people in your life may seem like they to want to do all they can to stop you from becoming a better YOU. They will express concern, they will shame, and they will sabotage your efforts to improve. Again, this is just human nature. Some of it is well-intentioned, but some of it is petty and immature projection of their own failings in life. Most of the people impeding your success will be those closest to you. Some of the hardest work you will have to do will be to step over and around them without alienating them completely. Sometimes that is impossible, and the only proper course of action is to remove them from your life completely. This is one of the toughest things a typical nice guy can do in life, but it is so very worth it, as every successful person will tell you. Life is short, and there is no room for toxic people on your road to happiness and fulfillment.

THE WELL-INTENTIONED WORRIERS

Here's a very real-world scenario: Your little sister loves talking about you to her friends and neighbors whenever she gets the chance. If you're at a social gathering with her, she will quickly grab you by the arm and bring you over to her friends, as if showing off her prize possession. *"This is*

George. He's my big bro I was telling you guys about!" What's she so happy about? Why is she so proud? Because her big bro is the nicest and sweetest guy on the planet Earth, of course. He's good with his kids, he's good with his siblings, he's good to his wife, and he's a really hard worker. She hopes to one day land a guy just like her big brother.

Your sister is closing in on thirty years of age, and she's growing tired of the conga line of *"cute but not husband material"* idiots that she meets online. After several one-night stands, lots of *"ghosting,"* and a few failed short-term relationships, your sister is more than a little pissed about the quality of the male dating pool available today. She considers her big brother to be the beacon of hope for women like her. It's good to see that sweet family guys still exist amongst the sea of dipshit losers she meets on a regular basis.

When little sister learns about your marriage breaking up, she is just as heart-broken as you are. Your ex becomes her sworn enemy for life. She will bad-mouth that woman at every opportunity. She seethes in anger when your divorce comes up. Doesn't that dumb cow of a woman realize what a perfect guy she had!? How dare she hurt her big brother like this! *"Don't worry,"* she tells you over coffee one day. *"You'll find somebody else. There are a million women looking for a guy like you. Trust me. I know from experience."*

You take your sister's words to heart and feel extremely optimistic, even excited, about the world of dating that lies ahead of you. All the other women in your life say much the same thing as your sister: You will have NO problem finding a nice girl who is looking for somebody just like you. You're a diamond in the rough. *"Trust me,"* they all say. *"You'll have ZERO trouble."*

The problem? You quickly learn that they are all wrong.

You play the sweet, nice guy game for a while and get nowhere. Lots of expensive dates. Lots of dinners. Lots of pecks on the cheek and "good night" as the women go back to their apartments and don't invite you in. Your long texting conversations with the cute gals from Match.com go on for hours, but they come to an abrupt stop when you decide to escalate and sway them towards the topic of actually going on a date. You're a great buddy to many women you meet, but not boyfriend material, as one of your more honest female friends tells you. She's right. Going beyond the buddy phase is proving to be nearly impossible.

Then you get frustrated and start looking for advice. You come across books like this one, listen to some friends who have luck with women, or just naturally become a more selfish guy who's no longer so hung up on finding a woman. You have other missions and goals in life and decide to focus on them instead. Unbelievably, the sex life kicks into overdrive. You can't believe it yourself, sometimes. By not caring so much about dating, by focusing on yourself, and by not looking for the next Mrs. Right, you're able to meet your intimacy needs… and then some. That's when your sister wakes up, notices what you've been up to, and changes her tune.

Little sis doesn't like what she sees. She notices that you've lost weight, dress differently, drive a cooler car, and she saw you out with three different women over the past couple of months. It doesn't take long until she puts two and two together. You've become one of those *"player"* types that she meets again and again on Tinder and Match.com. *"Oh, no... not my perfect teddy bear of a brother!"*

Little sister is the perfect example of a well-intentioned, loving friend or family member that holds you up on the pedestal of being a really super nice person. They believe we live in a world of selfishness and shallowness, and it's nice to know that there are good people like you still out there. What they don't see is that you routinely get stepped on, taken advantage of, and sometimes abused all in the name of being a *"nice guy."* Ironically, people like your little sister repeatedly show through their own actions just how wrong they are about relationships. They really don't know a damn thing about the modern-day mating game as their lack of real and loving relationships so obviously shows.

Your sister is not alone in her worries. Your best friend Dustin and his wife are concerned, too. Dustin says you need to stop with dating around and meeting all these women for sex. He thinks you need to just grow up and go back to the old you. He sees value in settling down and working on a family. He sees what you are doing as *"giving up on the dream."* He tries to set you up with a single mom he knows who has four kids of her own. She's been unlucky in the dating department. She's vocal about finding a great guy to settle down with. You politely decline. This really pisses

Dustin off. *"You can't go on pretending to be Mr. Playboy forever. Eventually, you're going to want to marry again, and it will be too late."* It's obvious that his wife's female-centric point of view (time being a major factor) has now infected your buddy's perspective.

You listen to his concerns, because he is your best friend and he means well, but Dustin's attitude gets on your damn nerves. You eventually reach the end of your rope and point out the obvious giant elephant in the room: He's not in a happy marriage. Not at all. Of all your married friends, Dustin is probably the most miserable and stereotypical Provider of them all. You let him have it. *"Oh yeah? How's that working out for you, exactly? Didn't you tell me you two haven't had sex in months, your wife won't give you blow-jobs, and all she does is complain about being fat and shows she hates her body? Weren't you caught looking at porn not once, not twice, but three times? Didn't she get so pissed that she bought you a book about porn addiction? Isn't that what you just told me a couple of weeks ago when you came over for beers? Why in the hell would I dive headfirst back into that life? Been there, done that, got the divorce to prove it. I'm going to take my time and get shit straight for once in my life. I will not force a relationship just so I can be back in the same boat again."*

The well-intentioned worriers are always oblivious to their own faults. Your overweight mom is worried about your *"drastic"* weight loss and tries to get you to eat more. Your promiscuous sister who routinely turns down nice guys doesn't want you to be a Lover… like all the other guys she meets and gladly gives sex to. Your sexless best friend who hates his boring life says you should also just give up on dating and settle down like him. You'll see it again and again. They all mean well. They do legitimately worry about you and your well being. They are concerned about the changes they see. Yet, their thoughts and worries should be taken with a grain of salt. They're not people to look up to in the big relationship game.

Don't listen to life's losers, no matter how well-intentioned and based on love their criticisms are.

THE TRULY TOXIC

You're very strict about what you eat. You've lost thirty pounds, you're looking great, and you're getting compliments from everyone. Some people you know are asking you for advice on how they can look better and be healthier, too. You become the diet, workout, and weight loss guru to your little circle of friends and coworkers. Their positive feedback just gives you more energy to continue improving. The snowball effect of *"positive results = feedback = more positive results"* grows and grows. Things are great. And then… HE shows up. Your negative friend. *"Dude, why do you have to be such a pussy all the time? Some pizza and beer is not going to kill you."* Your friend is, of course, the quintessential *"Dad Bod."* He looks like a wad of bubble gum. Your improvements have given him a very real and candid look at what he COULD be with some discipline, honesty, and hard work. Instead, he goes with the flow and looks and feels like shit. You're making it very tough for him to live in the little cocoon of a world he has built for himself. He may have even caught his wife talking about you in glowing terms and now he feels threatened. He feels that by putting you down and sabotaging your efforts, he is in-turn elevating himself. He's an asshole. Avoid him at all costs.

Let's say you're at a party with friends. It's been about a year since you divorced from your ex, and you've been feeling out the dating scene for the past couple of months. Lucky for you, you've had success with ladies of all ages and backgrounds. Your married friends live vicariously through the stories you tell of sneaking off with that gal from the coffee shop, the making out with the single MILF from the PTO meetings, the love-struck college girl who won't stop texting you, the forty-something gal from your office, etc. One guy from your friend group, though, doesn't take your changes too well. He's what they call the quintessential *"White Knight."* He takes it upon himself to stand up for the perceived damsels in distress at every opportunity. He's never met a woman he didn't put on the highest of pedestals. While most of your friends are saying that you're lucky to be getting attention from all these women, the White Knight will say that you're just taking advantage of their vulnerable states and you should stop being a such a typical male predator. Nothing you or your other friends say will change his mind. As far as he's concerned, you represent all that is wrong with men today. Basically, he's a little worm who can't get women and the sexual relationship he desires. He resents those men that have success. His jumping on the *"team woman"* bandwagon is actually an underhanded and dishonest way of trying to get laid. *"If I become a super-fem-*

inist, pro-female, anti-male type of man… then women will love me more." He's obviously wrong and he will drive himself insane with his lack of real results in life. Avoid him before his toxic ways rub off on you.

The well-intentioned can be turned around by showing them the true and positive motivations behind your changes. They're good people that are just looking out for your safety and don't want to see you get hurt. They also don't want to see you transform into something they see as truly negative. Their feelings are genuine, but that doesn't mean they aren't based on their own inadequacies. Simply maintain your mission and be there for them when they finally wake up and ask you for help in their own journeys towards self-improvement (which happens more often than not).

The toxic should be avoided at all costs. Nothing you say or do will transform their thinking. You shouldn't be caught up in the game of trying to win them over. The more you play into their game, the more negative you and they both become. You should instead limit as much of your time with them as possible. If possible, erase them from your life. Let them crawl back to you later. Even then, keep them at a safe distance.

Any successful man ever will tell you the same thing: As soon as you realize your potential and start making drastic improvements to your life, the losers come out of the woodwork to pull you back down to their level. Shitty people just love to try to bring others down with them. It's just an interesting quirk of human nature.

YOUR HABITS

Your habits are all those things you do on a regular basis without even thinking about them. They are actions that, because of their repetition, have just become a normal part of your day-to-day existence. They're now part of your autonomous mental programming. Many habits, as we know, are not good for you. A habit of reaching for a cigarette first thing in the morning: Not good. A habit of eating a giant fattening breakfast every morning: Not good. A habit of going out drinking after work every day with your buddies: Not good.

It took one simple decision, and many days of repetition to get these habits programmed into your brain. Some habits, like cigarettes and alcohol, became habitual because of their addictive chemical compositions. After all, they were specifically designed and engineered to make you feel great for a short amount of time and then keep you coming back for more. There's also a social component to drinking and smoking that makes them more enjoyable and further embeds the habitual programming into your psyche. If you're happy and laughing with friends while doing it, then you're more likely to continue the behavior, lungs and liver be damned.

Other habits aren't necessarily healthy or unhealthy, but just by doing them again and again, they became etched into your brain. If you hang around people long enough, you recognize their own little unique habits. Years ago, I had a coworker who had a completely unconscious ritual that he did multiple times a day. He would sit down in his office chair, grunt, grab the computer mouse, tap it twice on the desk, and then move the mouse rapidly back and forth. This was his way of *"waking up"* his computer so that he could start working. He did this every single day, multiple times a day. I didn't have to look over the cubicle wall to see if he was there. I could sit and wait for the telltale *"grunt, tap tap, mouse-scraping"* noise ritual. If you asked my coworker about his grunting, tapping mouse routine, he would have had no idea what in the hell you were talking about. It was all automatic. He unwittingly programmed this series of actions into his day-to-day routine. To him, it was like blinking. (Now you're thinking about blinking. Sorry.)

An important key to getting over the hump in life and really achieving self-improvement is to understand and harness the power of this automated habit system we have built into all of our brains. Get control of your habits, and things happen much easier for you.

The process is two-fold:

1. Eliminate old habits that keep you from reaching your goals.

2. Do little things every day that help you achieve your goals and do them until they become habits.

I think it's important that you sit down and take an inventory of your day-to-day activities. Write it all down. Every little stupid detail, no matter how trivial, you write it down.

If you're a complete physical disaster, your daily itinerary may look something like this:

• Wake up. Hit snooze three or four times. Eventually, get out of bed. Brush teeth. Smoke a cigarette. Drink coffee. Eat cereal. Take a shower. Put on clothes. Drive to work.

• Eat a donut or two at the office. Talk to coworkers during a cigarette break.

• Eat lunch at a pub with coworkers. Burger and fries, usually. Have a beer with the meal. Smoke a cigarette afterward.

• Another cigarette break.

• Leave work. Head to the pub for a few drinks (and maybe some unhealthy food) and have at least two more   cigarettes.

• Go home. Eat something. Usually something frozen or leftovers from the previous night. Maybe get fast food on the way home. Watch TV. Another cigarette.

• Take the laptop to bed. Watch Netflix or browse the internet until you fall asleep.

In the pitiful, but unfortunately realistic list above, it's pretty obvious which habits should be immediately eliminated. Smoking and drinking stick out from the list along with unhealthy eating, but so does hitting the snooze button repeatedly, going home to watch TV, and internet surfing before bed. Like for most people, there is a lot of room for improvement, and it starts one habit at a time.

It's time that you identify the little day-to-day habits that need improving and do something in their place that is more positive and productive. How long until those new things become habits that you don't even need to think about? Approximately two months. Yes, you need to do something for two months before your brain finally says, *"I guess we'll be filing this away in the unconscious mind and do them automatically, since it's so important to you."* That's when it finally clicks.

Examples of habits from the above list that can be changed:

• Instead of hitting the snooze button, you jump out of bed immediately, quickly stretch, let out a big grunt, and run to the bathroom to take a shower.

• Instead of eating cereal, you skip breakfast and drink coffee (thanks to your intermittent fasting routine), or eat something healthy, like fruit and eggs.

• Instead of taking cigarette breaks with coworkers, you spend the additional time doing something more pro-ductive that will help your work, or take a timeout to read something you enjoy.

• Instead of going to the pub for lunch, you bring something healthy from home and eat at your desk, or you go outside to sit in the sun and eat and chat with coworkers that also brought their lunches to work.

• Instead of hitting the pub right after work, you go to the gym.

• You go to the grocery store after the gym and grab something healthy to make for dinner and for your lunches during the week.

• You eat dinner and enjoy some downtime.

• Instead of taking your laptop to bed, you read a book and fall asleep at a decent time, getting as close to eight hours of sleep as possible.

That sounds far more productive and healthier than the alternative, but it's also difficult to do. It can all be too much to tackle at once. I recommend you first do the obvious and eliminate the health-killing vices like alcohol and cigarettes as step number one. Put something else in their place immediately. Give it two months to really sink in and make a difference.

Once those big vices are eliminated and replaced with new, healthier habits for two months, you can then start adding on additional positive habits, but not before then. You don't want to make the common mistake of overwhelming yourself with too many life changes and lose something important in the shuffle. If you throw too much on your plate at first, you will fail. People respond better to little changes over time.

Here are some additional items you can add to your arsenal of habits. These will all pay positive dividends down the line:

1. Go for a walk every morning.
2. Drink lots of water throughout the day.
3. Eat only fresh foods.
4. Read every day.
5. Keep a journal of thoughts and ideas.
6. Stretch every day.
7. Clean your home every day.
8. Check your personal finances every day.
9. Talk to a friend every day.
10. Do something that makes money every day.

Every one of these habits is a step towards feeling, looking, and DOING better. They all have a purpose. They're all part of a larger state of mind called "discipline." While eating pizza and staying up late watching Netflix sounds great, it doesn't do a damn thing for you. In fact, it will only help you add on weight and deprive you of the much-needed sleep you must have to function properly.

There's a helpful mantra by former Navy Seal and motivational speaker Jocko Willink:

"Discipline Equals Freedom."

The only way to get to the coveted goal of true freedom is to have discipline in all facets of life. If you want financial freedom, then you need to take control of your finances. Don't spend frivolously. Save. Pay off debt. If you want the physical freedom that good health and energy provide, then you need the discipline to put down the snacks and beer and instead eat real foods and hit the gym. If you want the freedom of living life on your terms and the freedom to hit your goals, you say NO to the insanely hot but obviously mentally ill woman that keeps texting you. You let somebody else play the part of savior and you focus on you, instead.

The same principles apply to life while you ARE in a good relationship with a genuinely good person. You use your discipline to set time for yourself and for your time together as a couple. You learn to say no to temptations and temporary pleasures that cause years of pain down the line. You recognize that a relationship is hard work, and you don't give in to the notion that it *"just happens."*

Get off your ass and do something positive. You're worth it.

EPILOGUE

263

I often say you shouldn't let trauma define you as a person. This is coming from the guy who started a website, podcast, wrote four books, has hundreds of articles, a YouTube channel, and an international men's group, and offers one-on-one coaching… all because my wife left me after a twenty-year relationship. Obviously, this was a traumatic and life-changing experience for me. But I could've taken this in an entirely different direction. I could've started up drinking way too much. I could've said to hell with it and gained a hundred pounds. I could've just told my ex to take the kids full time and ran off to California to live as a beach bum. I could've continued sleeping around with attractive but mentally ill women who would've made my life a lot more difficult.

Life gave me a pot full of disgusting ingredients to work with, and I've done my best to make a tasty stew out of it. I could've REALLY fucked up in a big way VERY easily. It took a lot of work to make sure I didn't. The work was well worth it.

I hope you don't take from this book an *"anti-relationship"* theme. I hope you don't come away thinking *"all women are whores"* after reading this. That's far from my intention. Relationships and women CAN be amazing. They can truly add to your life in immeasurable ways. I truly love my wife with all of my heart, and respect her a great deal as a human being. She's proven to be a fantastic person and one I am happy to go through life with. I am looking forward to our many years together.

As science shows us, human animals gravitate towards pair-bonding. Even the manliest testosterone-fueled maniac has a woman on the back of his motorcycle. We all innately seem to know that going through life alone is pretty damn tough. The problem is that nature also puts us in a state of mind that literally blinds us to faults that others around us see so clearly. Yes, that sexy blond makes you feel like king of the world, but she's jobless, has three kids, was once on heroin, used to have an eating disorder, and she may or may not have been a sex worker in the past… depending on who you ask. That is not a good relationship candidate. That is somebody you need to stay the hell away from.

Your partner may be out there waiting, but you may not find her. That's okay. You'll be okay on your own. In fact, you're never on your own. You have a brotherhood of men out there that are more than willing to extend a helping hand. The world is your oyster, my friend. Go out and make a new social group and help others in need. Get to work on yourself.

"Treat yourself like someone you are responsible for helping."
   –   Dr. Jordan B. Peterson

Things will work out in the end. It's all up to you. Make it happen.

JOIN US!

Join hundreds of men in your shoes from all over the world in our private group for men only: **HFM Brotherhood.** We have live group meetings (all recorded to listen to later), private online discussion groups, members-only articles, a members-only podcast, big discounts on one-on-one coaching, and live in-person meetups. We would love to see you in the group and look forward to helping you and learning what we can from your own experience. Join us!

helpformen.com/join

REFERENCES

Glover, Dr. Robert. No More Mr. Nice Guy. Running Press, 2003.

Korb, Alex. Empty Man Syndrome, Why Some Men Get Stuck in Depression. Psychology Today, March 1, 2015, https://www.psychologytoday.com/ca/blog/prefrontal-nudity/201503/empty-man-syndrome.

McDonald, Lyle. The Stubborn Fat Solution. Body Recomposition, 2008.

Peterson, Dr. Jordan B. Modern Times: Camille Paglia & Jordan B Peterson. Jordan B Peterson, October 2, 2017, https://www.youtube.com/watch?v=v-hIVnmUdXM.

Willink, Jocko. Discipline Equals Freedom (Jocko Willink Motivation). HESMotivation, https://www.youtube.com/results?search_query=discipline+equals+freedom

DIVORCE PANIC

http://www.helpformen.com

© 2022 D.S.O.
All rights reserved. No portion of this book may be repro-
duced in any form without permission from the publisher,
except as permitted by U.S. copyright law.

For permissions contact:
ralph.b@helpformen.com

Cover by Ralph B.

www.ingramcontent.com/pod-product-compliance
Lightning Source LLC
Chambersburg PA
CBHW070506160726
48003CB00004B/1451